STAND UP!

STAND UP!

Fearless Women in the Gospel of Mark

JOHANNES ECKERT, OSB

Paulist Press
New York / Mahwah, NJ

Cover images: Front/back cover image of women raising joined hands by Jasmina007/iStock.com; background texture by Nagib/Shutterstock.com
Cover design by Sharyn Banks
Book design by Lynn Else

Originally published as *Steht auf! Frauen im Markus-Evangelium als Provokation für heute*, copyright © 2018 Verlag Herder GmbH, Freiburg im Breisgau
Translated by Nancy de Flon. Copyright © 2021 by Paulist Press, Inc.

Library of Congress Cataloging-in-Publication Data
Names: Eckert, Johannes, 1969– author. | de Flon, Nancy Marie, translator.
Title: Stand up! : fearless women in the Gospel of Mark / Johannes Eckert, OSB ; translated by Nancy de Flon.
Other titles: Steht auf English
Description: New York / Mahwah : Paulist Press, 2021. | "Originally published as *Steht auf Frauen im Markus-Evangelium als Provokation für heute*, copyright 2018, Verlag Herder GmbH, Freiburg im Breisgau." | Summary: "An unconventional look at, and biblical search for, six nameless women of the Bible and their stirring message for today"—Provided by publisher.
Identifiers: LCCN 2020018922 | ISBN 9780809155040 (paperback)
Subjects: LCSH: Women in the Bible. | Bible. Mark—Criticism, interpretation, etc.
Classification: LCC BS2445 .E3513 2021 | DDC 226.3/0922082—dc23
LC record available at https://lccn.loc.gov/2020018922

ISBN 978-0-8091-5504-0 (paperback)

English edition published by Paulist Press
997 Macarthur Boulevard
Mahwah, New Jersey 07430
www.paulistpress.com

Printed and bound in the
United States of America

CONTENTS

INTRODUCTION

Provoked by the Gospel...

"Stand up!" That brief appeal resembles a call to insurrection and recalls the beginning of the left-wing anthem the "Internationale": "Arise, all victims of oppression!" But it could also be the title of a children's song with which my niece loves to wake up her parents. A rough translation of the German song is, "You sleeper, you tardy one, you sleepyhead, you groundhog!—Stand up!" Even when we are lovingly awakened, it's sometimes difficult to stand up. We don't want to get out of a warm bed—we'd prefer to stay under the covers a bit longer. The process can also have its unpleasant aspects: The shrill sound of the alarm jars you from your sleep. Startled, you sit up in bed and hear the call, "Stand up!" Likewise, we can have a figurative "awakening"—through an unexpected encounter, a tragic stroke of fate, or a surprising turn of events.

Nothing else describes the word *provocation*. It comes from the Latin *pro-vocare* and means "to goad, to incite, to rouse, to egg on, to awaken." A provocation will often awaken us, summon us out of our well-ordered world, and open our eyes to what is essential. It will incite us to resistance by depicting familiar situations in deliberately distorted or exaggerated ways.

Understood in that way, Mark's Gospel, which probably appeared around AD 70 and is thus the oldest of the four Gospels, must have been a real provocation for its earliest readers, who had yet to be exposed to the Christian faith. How could the story of the life and sufferings of an insignificant man despised by the religious leaders of his people and publicly crucified as a criminal by the Roman occupying power, a man from Nazareth in Galilee, an unknown hole at the outskirts of the Roman empire, be titled *Evangelium*, "Gospel," which means "good news"? Originally the concept of *evangelium* designated a message of glad tidings from the emperor and was generally used in the plural. Examples of such "glad tidings," which were proclaimed throughout the entire Roman empire, might be victories over enemy armies, announcements about taxes being lowered, or the birth of a potential heir to the throne. What does all of this have to do with a crucified Galilean?

Mark the evangelist is the first author to speak of *evangelium* in the singular, and thereby—consciously or otherwise—he created a new literary genre. In the process, however, he certainly did not compose a work with a happy ending (see Mark 16:1–8). In his original closing scene, three women come to Jesus's tomb on the Sunday after the crucifixion, intending to anoint his body. There they encounter a man in a white garment, an angel, who announces to them that the Crucified One has risen and has gone before his disciples to Galilee. The women are to report this to Peter and his companions. One might assume that the women would rejoice over the surprisingly positive turn of events—but no: they leave the tomb overcome with fear and dismay and tell no one about what has happened. No trace of Easter celebration or resurrection joy here! Mark's Gospel ends with silence and shock!

This so-called open ending is a provocation in the truest sense of the word. Inevitably, the reader must ask, What does this mean? What reactions does the evangelist want to awaken? What happened to the women after this?

Subsequent generations did not tolerate the "open ending." With the help of the Gospels of Matthew and Luke, which came later, they crafted a "happy ending" that makes everything turn out fine (see Mark 16:9–20). But in so doing they weakened, even falsified, the message of the first evangelist.

In the original ending, the women take on a key role, particularly since the Gospel says nothing more about the disciples after Jesus was arrested (see Mark 14:50). The women in Mark's account, however, are like a silk thread on which the future of his work crucially depends. The evangelist has already mentioned them earlier, in the passion narrative. In order to understand how provocative the open ending is, it helps first to look at this brief scene in order then to devote oneself more intensively to the Easter story.

...BY EXEMPLARY WOMEN...

> When it was noon, darkness came over the whole land until three in the afternoon. At three o'clock Jesus cried out with a loud voice, "Eloi, Eloi, lema sabachthani?" which means, "My God, my God, why have you forsaken me?" When some of the bystanders heard it, they said, "Listen, he is calling for Elijah." And someone ran, filled a sponge with sour wine, put it on a stick, and gave it to him to drink, saying, "Wait, let us see whether Elijah will come to take him down." Then Jesus gave a loud cry and breathed his last. And the curtain of the temple was torn in two, from top to bottom. Now when the centurion, who stood facing him, saw that in this way he breathed his last, he said, "Truly this man was God's Son!"
>
> There were also women looking on from a distance; among them were Mary Magdalene, and Mary the mother of James the younger and of Joses, and

> Salome. These used to follow him and provided for him when he was in Galilee; and there were many other women who had come up with him to Jerusalem. (Mark 15:33–41)

The gruesome death scene in the crucifixion story is dominated by the impressive confession of the pagan centurion: "Truly this man was God's Son!" (Mark 15:39). He is the only person in Mark's Gospel who puts into words who this man from Nazareth really is: the Son of God! Just as remarkable is the fearless presence of the women who witness the sad event on the cross. Where did the men go whom Jesus invited into his close entourage in Galilee and who set off with him in Galilee? What has become of Peter, James, and John, who were exclusively allowed to accompany Jesus in special moments, such as the revival of a deceased little girl, or the transfiguration on the mountain, or in the garden of Gethsemane on the night before his death? About the disciples after the arrest of Jesus, Mark comments tersely and succinctly: "All of them deserted him and fled" (Mark 14:50).

The women, in contrast, courageously remain steadfastly faithful to Jesus until his death. Already in Galilee, they had followed him and served him, as the evangelist reports. By his reference both to "follow" and to "serve," Mark emphasizes that these women, through their model behavior, show themselves to be authentic disciples—and indeed that they are totally worthy of being numbered among the community of disciples! The death scene demonstrates this in an impressive way: to follow means that they confess Jesus in word and in deed. The proper attitude of the women is one of a piece with the confession of faith expressed by the centurion. They are "upstanding women" in the truest sense of the term because discipleship means to put your own life at risk for Jesus, even when you are "only" looking on from a distance.

Three women—Mary of Magdala, Mary the mother of James and Joses, and Salome—are named by Mark. Two of them then become witnesses at the tomb (see Mark 15:47) and all three come to the tomb on Easter morning (see Mark 16:1–8). In addition to these women, Mark mentions still other anonymous female disciples who have accompanied Jesus on the journey from Galilee to Jerusalem.

It's intriguing to pursue this two-pronged trail that Mark creates in the crucifixion scene. Two sets of questions arise from it. First, what do the women who are the above-named Easter messengers have to say to the reader? What do they want to provoke in the reader? Second, it's just as exciting to follow the trail of the women whom the Gospel doesn't name: Where did they crop up? How do they set an example? What message do they have for us today?

At this point it would be well first to consider in still more detail Mark's open ending, which can also be read as a prologue to the entire Gospel.

...WITH FAITH IN THE EASTER MESSAGE...

> When the sabbath was over, Mary Magdalene, and Mary the mother of James, and Salome bought spices, so that they might go and anoint him. And very early on the first day of the week, when the sun had risen, they went to the tomb. They had been saying to one another, "Who will roll away the stone for us from the entrance to the tomb?" When they looked up, they saw that the stone, which was very large, had already been rolled back. As they entered the tomb, they saw a young man, dressed in a white robe, sitting on the right side; and they were alarmed. But he said to them, "Do not be alarmed; you are looking for Jesus of Nazareth, who was crucified. He has been raised; he is not

> here. Look, there is the place they laid him. But go, tell his disciples and Peter that he is going ahead of you to Galilee; there you will see him, just as he told you." So they went out and fled from the tomb, for terror and amazement had seized them; and they said nothing to anyone, for they were afraid. (Mark 16:1–8)

Sometimes I ask myself how my life would be if I had never heard anything about this Jesus of Nazareth and his resurrection. Or: How would our world look today if the women had remained silent? Mark, with his open ending, challenges his readers to look more intently at the Easter tidings of the young man at the tomb. How would I have reacted had I been in the place of the women?

This extraordinary tomb story is about the women reorienting themselves. We could also say that they are challenged to conversion. In a sense, they were confronted with this challenge with the first words that Jesus speaks in Mark's Gospel: "The time is fulfilled, and the kingdom of God has come near; repent, and believe in the good news" (Mark 1:15). What does this mean?

After the horrific events of Good Friday that the three women have experienced up close, they go early in the morning to the tomb to anoint Jesus's body. After three days it is too late for this. At the same time, the attentive reader knows that Jesus was anointed by a woman for his burial already at the beginning of his passion (see Mark 14:3–9). Let us look more closely at this scene. If, now, the three women want to complete the anointing of the corpse, then in no way are they coming to the tomb in hopes of a resurrection. It's much more likely that they accept the sad certainty: "Dead is dead!" Now it is their sorrowful task to perform for the corpse the final act of loving service. That is their frame of mind when they are thinking about who can roll away the stone for them at the tomb.

The evangelist, however, gently paints another picture: While at the hour of Jesus's death on Good Friday a darkness spreads over the land and overshadows the crucifixion as a grim scenario, now, very early on Easter day, the sun rises. The light conquers the night of death. It dawns slowly. Likewise, something dawns on the women while they ask, "Who will roll away the stone for us?" This can be understood figuratively: "Who will free us from the burden of death?" This question is certainly familiar to everyone who has had to say goodbye to someone they love. Like a boulder, sorrow can be a heavy burden on our heart.

The surprising evidence that the enormous stone is already rolled away is a further indication of the change of perspective that the reader should undergo together with the women. The burden of death is rolled away and the tomb stands open.

Inside, the women meet a young man in a white garment that reminds us of Jesus's transfiguration in Galilee (Mark 9:2–10). There his disciples Peter, James, and John saw him in brilliant light and in a white garment. Already on that occasion it became clear where his journey would lead: into the light-filled world of God! Now the women are confronted with the existence of God, and they react with fear and amazement. In the biblical context this is not uncommon but, rather, typical for an encounter with the Divine. Ultimately, they experience, in the young man, the closeness of the kingdom of God. Now the time is really fulfilled, as Jesus had proclaimed when he first emerged on the scene. And that is also the message that the young man proclaims to them: "The Crucified One has been risen!" God has brought Jesus of Nazareth into a new dimension of life. The beloved Son, as the Father bore witness during his baptism in the Jordan and on the mountain of the transfiguration, and as which the centurion recognized him in the Crucified One, can't possibly remain in the realm of the dead. He is not here—that is, the tomb, the world of death, is no longer the space in which Jesus is to be found! Here is not where the women are to seek him. On the contrary: they are charged with turning away from the tomb and going to the men who fled in fright (Mark 14:50), even to Peter, who had denied him (Mark 14:66–72). The women were to announce to them, "He is going ahead of you to Galilee" (Mark 16:7).

Viewed through a sociocultural lens, the angel's commission is provocative, considering that women are subordinate to men in the ancient world. Also, they are not to speak publicly. Yet, in the Gospel of Mark the angel commissions them to do exactly that: They are not to remain silent at the tomb but to proclaim the good news. They themselves are to be God's messengers, that is, to become angels who serve the gospel!

Actually, the women had been looking in the wrong place and are now set on the right track. The joyful message is meant for them, too, since it says, "He is going ahead of you," and not, "He is going ahead of them [the men]!" The Risen One goes ahead of the women, too, and, along with them, ahead of us, the readers of the Gospel. As the women turn around and leave the tomb behind, they reach out toward what lies ahead of them.

That, too, is a clear wake-up call to the reader. During our lives much may indeed pursue us or follow behind us if we, like the women, experience something shocking. But the Risen One goes not behind us but ahead of us! And he doesn't pursue us the way encounters or experiences in our life story sometimes pursue us and refuse to let go. Rather, he summons us to "follow after" to Galilee and challenges us to follow in his footsteps, to incorporate them in our life, and to follow after him the way we pursue something that interests us and about which we wish to learn more! Also, the Risen One doesn't return to the home from which he came. No, he goes ahead, that is, he goes before his disciples into Galilee, or, as we could also put it, he is the future in person. There in Galilee, where everything began, is where the women are to meet him—there is where their lives receive a future. With these three women and their mission of proclamation, God begins anew. If the Risen One goes ahead to Galilee, then this, at the end of the Gospel, is a challenge to read this again and to ask, What has this to do with my life? Where do I encounter the Risen One in the story of my life and my faith, in the concreteness of my every day? In my Galilee? Where do I find his tracks, where does he go before me? Our life is the place where we discover the Good News.

...TO TURN AROUND AND FOLLOW THE RISEN ONE!

Considering this, one cannot finish reading Mark's Gospel and then simply snap the book shut and go back to one's daily business. At the end it becomes clear why Mark begins his work with these words: "The beginning of the good news of Jesus Christ" (Mark 1:1). The evangelist establishes a beginning in such a way that the life of the reader is the continuation and becomes the real gospel. His book resembles an overture in which the important motifs are already sounding. But the real opera, the main work, is nothing other than our life. In this sense it is for us to take up the Easter melody and let it play out as a leitmotiv in all its glory and in manifold variations. Mark has written only a prologue—the real work is written by us. In that we follow after Jesus and, like the three women, set out with him on the journey, in that we listen to his word and are prepared to serve him, our life becomes a continuation of the Gospel. This is how we can encounter the Risen One. To begin the open ending anew is an encouragement for each person: for the women who fall silent, for the disciples who have all run away, for Peter who has denied Jesus, and for each person who is plagued by doubts about their faith and is confronted with the tomb, that is, with the power of death. Again and again, God makes possible a new beginning.

Whoever is, in contrast, fixated only on the empty tomb sees only where Jesus is *not* to be found. Whoever wants to encounter him, however, must turn around with the women and embark on the path of the Living One.

This is the task of the church in our time. How often do we fix our gaze on that which once was and is no more? How often do we persist in sorrow over what is in the past and wallow in a nostalgic backward look to a time in which everything, apparently, was better? That is understandable, and indeed the church is founded on a great tradition that provides much support and certainty. But the perspective offered by Mark's Gospel is different: "Don't look back—instead look to what lies ahead of you!" it bids us.

"He is going ahead of you to Galilee!" Mark's Gospel calls us to turn from the past, to change our perspective, to look ahead, to turn toward the future and thus to the Risen One. Jesus's proclamation is meant for us, too: "The time is fulfilled, and the kingdom of God has come near; repent, and believe in the good news" (Mark 1:15).

In the Greek text the word used here for "time" is not *chronos*, which refers to the passage of time, the chronology of events. Instead the word is *Kairos*. In Greek mythology the demigod Kairos represented the favorable moment that had to be seized while the opportunity was there. Because of this, he was depicted in art as a bald youth with a shock of hair on his forehead. Thus, whoever is too late in taking the initiative and does not seize the opportunity with both hands comes up empty.

Jesus challenges us not to mourn for the "good old days" but to recognize the favorable moment. The three women have seemingly understood and proclaimed this, otherwise neither Mark nor we would ever have heard the Easter message. After their initial fright, they probably overcame their speechlessness and plunged into the future that lay before them. Mark's Gospel doesn't tell us whether they really encountered the Risen One in Galilee. But by leaving the tomb and setting out for Galilee—in other words, into life—the women were aware that Jesus was going before them and so was showing them the journey through their life.

As already mentioned, some other unnamed women are

standing with these three women by the cross. About them Mark says that they had accompanied Jesus from Galilee to Jerusalem. In their lifestyle and their faith, they were model disciples. We know nothing more about them.

A closer reading of the Gospel of Mark reveals six passages in which Jesus encounters women who are not named. Their behavior is consistently presented as a model for the disciples. Whether they have anything to do with the women standing at the cross is not revealed to us, but we associate them with these women because of their model conduct.

Has Mark forgotten their names, or did he consider their names irrelevant? We don't know that either. But perhaps our own experience can help us here. When we can't remember a name, then we describe the person: "What's the name of the woman who is always so well dressed, is so friendly, and lives on the third floor of the house on the corner?" For the most part, through the description we know more about the person than if we simply remembered their name.

Even if the six women in the Gospel remain anonymous, they were in no way insignificant or indeed without effect. They, too, were "upstanding women" who, through their portrayal here, show the reader how a person can follow Jesus and be his disciple. On closer inspection, all these scenes are Easter scenes that can provoke even today's community of disciples—in other words, the church—to resurrection. Thus, it will repay itself to consider them more intensely and to reflect on what new beginnings these anonymous women can lead us: What have they to say to us today? Where must we turn around, leave the past behind us, and orient ourselves in a new direction? Where can their example awaken new life in the church?

When I began preparing this book it was, first, very helpful for me to make direct contact with these six anonymous women. I began to write them letters, to ask them personally about their experiences, and to tell them about our time and the challenges we face. This, in turn, resulted in these women coming to life in my thoughts and becoming concrete persons, so that we began an imaginary dialogue with one another. In their written replies, they subjected conditions in today's church to critical questioning based on their own experiences. On the one hand this was very exciting, but on the other hand it was not always pleasant. Now and then they could make me quite uncomfortable. Thus, it became clear to me that we "men of the church" cannot evade these female figures and their critical mirror. Jesus's disciples didn't fare any differently. The women encourage reflection about conditions in the church: What is in accord with the gospel? Where are conversion and new beginnings mentioned? What could be changed? The women are performing an essential service for the church with this "wake-up call." After all, the Greek word for church, *ekklesia*, does mean "those who have been called"! By this is meant everyone who is called by Jesus through his gospel into a new way of living. It is quite in this sense that the six female figures provoke us to wake up, by shouting out to us with my niece's words: "Stand up!"

Chapter 1

A WOMAN SERVES AUTHENTICALLY

Almost twenty-five years ago we took a survey of the visitors to our brewpub in Andechs in southern Germany. With reference to the Benedictine motto *Ora et labora* (pray and work), one of the questions was "Did you know that monks live and work in Andechs?" A visitor with a sense of humor offered this feedback: "Knew that they lived, work is new to me!" Of course, the response contained some concealed criticism that more or less means this: So that the monks can live good lives, others must work for them!

This reminded me of stories from before the Second Vatican Council. At that time, which I did not personally experience, our monasteries were two-tiered societies. Back then, choir monks (who were priests) and brothers (who were not) had different statuses. The abbot and the choir monks had the decision-making power. As clerics, they enjoyed many privileges and represented the community in the outside world. The brothers, on the other hand, had only a limited say in decisions. They were required to serve the higher-status choir monks by carrying out such household tasks as cleaning, cooking, laundry, and so forth, and by performing the (at times) heavy physical agricultural labor and running the businesses. While the choir monks sang the full Divine Office in Latin, the brothers prayed simpler prayers in German. The differences between choir monks and brothers even extended to the quality of the meals, which the two groups ate separately. For example, for breakfast the brothers only got malt coffee (a barley drink), while the choir monks enjoyed real coffee made from coffee beans. The list of differences goes on.

Thank God, this unpleasant two-tiered society ended through the reforms of Vatican II. This was in keeping with the ideal of the *Rule of St. Benedict*. Benedict warns against some priests in the community enjoying privileges or a position of primacy (see RB 60; 62). Rather, he follows the ideal of the ancient church when, in a chapter on kitchen service, he establishes: "The brothers should serve one another" (RB 35.1). This is a central thought of the *Rule*, which states a basic point about following Jesus. To be a Christian means to accept the other as he is, and to serve him impartially. Benedict emphasizes this matter when he writes that "the abbot should avoid all favoritism in the monastery" (RB 2.16).

This becomes clear right at the beginning of Mark's Gospel, when Jesus, on the first day he appears in public, raises up Simon's mother-in-law. After she is healed, she serves the guests in her house. In this way she exemplifies what it means to follow in Jesus's footsteps. Just as he was of service in her life, so, too, she is prepared to do the same for him.

THE RAISING OF SIMON'S MOTHER-IN-LAW

> As soon as they left the synagogue, they entered the house of Simon and Andrew, with James and John. Now Simon's mother-in-law was in bed with a fever, and they told him about her at once. He came and

> took her by the hand and lifted her up. Then the fever left her, and she began to serve them. (Mark 1:29–31)

Admittedly, I hadn't thought thoroughly about this passage in Mark's Gospel before or used it as a theme in a homily. It's short and easy to overlook. In focusing on it more intensively, it becomes clear that this inconspicuous healing story at the beginning of the Gospel corresponds with the scene at the tomb at the end, which we have already looked at. Let us consider it in more detail.

Jesus visits the village of Capernaum by the Sea of Gennesaret. Many exegetes translate this place name as "Village of Comfort." This could be a portent for the healings that Jesus will work here. The German word for comfort—*Trost*—and the English word *trust* derive from the word for faithfulness—*Treue*. God's comfort and faithfulness become visible through the actions of his Son. Earlier, Jesus had encountered some young men at the seashore. "Follow me and I will make you fish for people," he called out to the brothers Simon and Andrew (Mark 1:17). They immediately leave their nets behind and follow him. Another pair of brothers, James and John, do the same. They promptly leave their father, Zebedee, behind with his day workers and go with Jesus. Through these anecdotes the evangelist is saying something important about the life of a disciple: To follow means to let go and to set out unreservedly on the path with Jesus!

It is interesting that Jesus then went to the four young men's home village. Apparently, he wanted to see where his new companions came from. He certainly had no interest in anything connected with family, origin, or upbringing.

After summoning this first group of disciples, Jesus attended the synagogue service on the following Sabbath. Here he worked his first healing miracle. A man who was possessed by an unclean spirit was freed from his agonizing suffering through Jesus's intervention. This public healing on a Sabbath was definitely a provocation, since no labor of any kind was allowed on this day of rest. Thus, right with his first miracle Jesus demonstrates what is decisive for him: First, he prioritizes the salvation and well-being of the human being above adherence to laws and regulations! This is what the art of fishing for people consists of. Consequently, as the Gospel continues, increasingly vehement conflicts arise between Jesus and the religious authorities of his day, so that Jesus expresses his conviction, stating, "The sabbath was made for humankind, and not humankind for the sabbath" (Mark 2:27). This saying was intended to provoke, and it did! To further emphasize this, Jesus repeatedly healed on the Sabbath, so that the Pharisees and Herod's adherents decided to kill him as soon as possible (see Mark 3:6).

From his very first healing in the synagogue in Capernaum, Jesus showed that when it came to people and their well-being, he was prepared to break with conventional precepts and to accept that conflicts would likely be a consequence. As a fisher of people, he put his life on the line for this message! His example is thus a guideline for the community of disciples in every age: The church exists to serve the people and their well-being!

But let's return to the healing that took place in the house of Simon and Andrew. After the public healing of a man, Mark now depicts the healing of a woman in the security of a private home. In this way Jesus makes one more important statement: He heals both sexes. He does not differentiate between man and woman.

The healing of Simon's mother-in-law is the shortest miracle story and, with a few deft strokes, so to speak, it draws attention to what is essential.

By his visit to the house of Simon and Andrew, Jesus enters the inner living space of his new companions. One almost wants to believe that he was introduced by them into their families and thereby shared in their everyday life.

The house in Capernaum will later be an important gathering place of the young Christian community. Toward the end of the first century it had become a meeting place and a worship space for the faithful. Later in Mark's Gospel, houses are preferred places for instructing new disciples. The house of Simon and Andrew in Capernaum is the first in a series of such houses.

In this house, Jesus learns that Simon's mother-in-law is in bed with a fever. At first, a fever may sound like an ordinary cold or flu. For pious Jews, however, every illness represented God's punishment, which meant further isolation and marginalization for the sick person. Mark expressly says that the mother-in-law was brought low, that is, powerless, weak, and dependent on help from others. Jesus shows interest in her and turns to her. Without words and without fear of contagion, he touches her, so that through him she experiences the closeness of God's kingdom. By taking her by the hand, he reveals himself as a fisher of people who pulls her up out of her fever and awakens her into new life. The Greek word *krateo* that Mark uses means "to seize" and comes from the word *kratos*—"power" and "strength." We could also say it this way: by touching her and raising her up, Jesus gives her power and strength and draws her into his life! Mark emphasizes that we have here a story with paschal overtones by using the Greek word *egeiro*—"to raise up," "to awaken." This corresponds with the angel's announcement to the astonished women by the empty tomb on Easter day: "He has been raised" (Mark 16:6). God has raised up his Son from death and given him new vitality. Simon's mother-in-law experiences something similar. When her fever breaks, she experiences her personal Easter, her awakening! She is, as it were, drawn by Jesus into his resurrection mystery or, we might also say, initiated into it.

The fever leaves her—or, literally, "lets go of her"—and she is freed from her illness. It is interesting that even in this context the talk is of "letting go." Previously, the four disciples had already let go of their nets and their father with his dayworkers. Just as they, having been embraced by Jesus's word, dare to make a break and to let go of everything, so, too, the mother-in-law has, in the truest sense, been embraced by Jesus's word so that she is "freed of her sickness" to follow Jesus and can serve him. Her reaction, described succinctly, says it all: "And she began to serve them"!

This is an imprecise translation because what is happening here isn't a one-time incident of hospitality in which a housewife goes into the kitchen to prepare a quick meal for her guests. The Greek word for "serve"—*diako*—is used here in the imperfect tense and describes an abiding attitude of service. The mother-in-law's example teaches the disciples and, along with them, us, the readers, what it means to emulate someone. To be grasped by Jesus means to serve! The woman who has been healed learns not by big words—not a single one is spoken in this scene—but by concrete deeds what it means to be awakened by Jesus, the fisher of people.

Later, shortly before his death, Jesus and his companions will once more be guests in a house in Capernaum (see Mark 9:33–37). We don't know whether it is the house belonging to Simon and Andrew, but the keyword *serve* recalls that house.

On the way there, the disciples are arguing about which of them is the most important. Consequently, when they reach their destination Jesus confronts them and rebukes them: "Whoever wants to be first must be last of all and servant of all" (Mark 9:35). Perhaps this reminded one or another of the disciples of the mother-in-law's service. But we don't find this out. To reinforce his words, Jesus will place a child in the midst of them, place his arms around the child, and say, "Whoever welcomes one such child in my name welcomes me, and whoever welcomes me welcomes not me but the one who sent me" (Mark 9:37). This is provocative, since in ancient societies women and children were considered second-class human beings. Jesus, in contrast, makes no such distinctions. Instead, he places himself on the same level as a child and in no uncertain terms points out that the acceptance of a child, that is, a second-class human being, leads to an encounter with God! All status distinctions are thereby abolished.

Then, as they continue their journey to Jerusalem, James and John will ask Jesus to reserve the best places in his future kingdom for them (see Mark 10:35–45). Understandably, this makes the other disciples angry. Once again Jesus has to teach them that to follow him has nothing to do with position and prestige, but with mutual service that ultimately means devotion. In the end his own journey would lead to Jerusalem, where he would give up his life on the cross. Referring to the common attitudes of the time, Jesus makes it clear: "You know that among the Gentiles those whom they recognize as their rulers lord it over them, and their great ones are tyrants over them. But it is not so among you; but whoever wishes to become great among you must be your servant, and whoever wishes to be first among you must be slave of all. For the Son of Man came not to be served but to serve, and to give his life a ransom for many" (Mark 10:42–45).

Discipleship is demonstrated essentially in service and in the devotion made visible by the mother-in-law's example. This is Jesus's teaching that Mark conveys to the community of disciples right at the beginning of his Gospel.

Service is mentioned in two further passages in Mark. It pays to look at them briefly as well. At the beginning of his public life, when Jesus withdraws to the desert, the Gospel reports that there in the desert—that is, in the place of death—angels served him (see Mark 1:13). These angels once again remind us of the angel at the tomb who announces that Jesus has risen. Now, if the angel and the mother-in-law serve Jesus, then they serve life and Easter, that is, resurrection, is proclaimed by their service.

Along with the angels in the desert and the mother-in-law in Capernaum, Mark's Gospel also mentions women who have served Jesus in Galilee and are witnesses to the crucifixion (see Mark 15:41). We have already met them in the introduction and can establish that their fearless faith is devotion that endures unto the end. They are "upstanding women" who, by their faithfulness and steadfastness, serve as models for the community of disciples.

Thus, we can summarize by saying that in Mark's Gospel it is solely angels and women who serve Jesus. That's a shameful resumé for the men. From this point of view, the healing of Simon's mother-in-law is not a small episode that Mark presents as an accessory to fill out his Gospel. Rather, it is a programmatic statement about Jesus's preaching. A person who is grasped by Jesus is called into his service. Simon's mother-in-law is the first disciple who follows Jesus through her exemplary behavior. She is initiated by him into his paschal mystery. This is something that the four who were called first—Simon, Andrew, James, and John—can learn from her. True discipleship is revealed through service, and the house in Capernaum thereby becomes a church, a house of comfort!

WILL ORDAINING WOMEN GIVE THE CHURCH MORE AUTHENTICITY?

"You are ordained to that which you already are!" With these lines a friend whose own priestly ordination had taken place many years earlier congratulated me on my ordination to the diaconate. These good wishes have stayed with me all this time. As a deacon and then a priest, I am consecrated to something that I already am. My friend was right. How many priestly and diaconal services are quite naturally performed by people who have not received a sacramental ordination but who have the charism? A simple example from my own experience may make this clear: As a child I often confessed to my parents what I had done in school. Of course, I was then still sent to confession, but the absolution and the reconciliation had already occurred. In the end it was my parents and many other models who, through their unselfish dedication, initiated me into priestly service, even though the official act took place through the bishop's prayer and laying on of hands.

"You are ordained to that which you already are!" Along with many men, it also occurs to me that many women in our parishes quite naturally perform diaconal and priestly services. I think of a female hospital chaplain whom I happened to meet when a young mother died. The entire family was gathered at the deathbed, full of sorrow and pain. The chaplain lovingly anointed with oil the young mother's forehead, eyes, ears, nose, mouth, hands, and feet, and, finally, her breast where her heart was. With her compassionate words she comforted the family members and helped them to say goodbye in a dignified way. One could feel how intensely she had accompanied the deceased woman on her final journey and prepared her for death. In this moment the hospital room became like the house in Capernaum, the place of comfort.

I also think of a female Catholic theologian who supported hospice workers in their demanding service of terminal care and regularly invited them to prayer services. Just a short time ago she received from a colleague, a self-described atheist, this compliment: "In you a pastor has been lost."

Similarly, many female counselors working in parish and other pastoral settings whom I got to know at celebrations of the sacrament of confirmation come to mind. Often these women are, for these young people, the first and only contact persons who understand their language and become involved in their world. For the *confirmandi*, who are sometimes far from the life of the church, they are the real pastors. Regardless of whether they are consecrated women, these young people confide their cares to them so that their confirmation preparation becomes the house in Capernaum.

The examples are many. I am concerned that many women suffer from the fact that they are refused the offices of deacon or priest. They perceive the church as a two-class society in which they are entrusted only with auxiliary work. Often they are highly qualified theologians and possess valuable charisms that they can only bring to the church in a limited way. How would Jesus react? Would he perhaps raise them up as he did Simon's mother-in-law and consecrate them in his service? Will we be able to explain to him why women are restricted in the ways they may serve in the house of the church, and do we men sometimes not resemble the disciples who did not understand much about discipleship?

One of the arguments against allowing women to be ordained deacons and priests is that Jesus himself was a man and that those who are ordained to represent him in the liturgy must act *in persona Christi*. In addition, Jesus invited only men into his inner circle. Finally, it is rather the social structure of that time to blame, in which women had no right to public witness. That they were devoted followers of Jesus is demonstrated by the scenes in the house in Capernaum and in Jesus's passion. It is all the more impressive that in Mark's Gospel it is precisely the women to whom Jesus drew close—Simon's mother-in-law is the very first person whom Jesus physically touches—and it is women who steadfastly remain near him during the crucifixion, while the male disciples couldn't get away fast enough. The women experienced Jesus's sacrifice on the cross up close. They became witnesses of his self-offering and were initiated into this event. Could they not, then, as servants of the faith, also preside at the Eucharist, the sacrament of the self-offering that makes Jesus's sacrifice on the cross present?

And what does it mean, anyway, to act *in persona Christi*? Isn't it more a matter of attitude than biological gender? Jesus Christ is the "Son of Man," as Mark refers to him in several passages. Man and woman with their dignity are equally incorporated into this human existence. They are enabled to represent Christ through their baptism in the name of Jesus Christ. This is encapsulated in the concept of the common priesthood of all the baptized, as declared by the Second Vatican Council.

Did Simon's mother-in-law not also act *in persona Christi* when she served in her house and thereby followed him who sought to serve humankind with his life, and who, out of love, even gave his life on the cross?

In our *Rule*, St. Benedict writes that the abbot of a monastery holds the place of Christ. He is to be the *vices Christi*—"Christ's representative" (RB 2.2). This is also true, of course, for each abbess in a cloister of nuns. Thus she, too, bears the staff and wears the ring and the pectoral cross as a sign of her service to Christ. Why, then, should she not also be ordained to exercise this service by administering the sacraments? Many find it difficult to comprehend, for example, that a community of sisters cannot celebrate daily Eucharist due to the lack of priests, although this is an essential basic element of the church. Naturally, this is true as well for the other sacraments. For some time, I have been serving a convent of sisters as confessor. Sometimes I ask myself whether it wouldn't be easier for these women to be able to discuss many topics with a woman. Or how helpful would it be if, for example, an abbess who has been serving her older, frail sisters could administer the sacrament of the sick to them?

In Simon's house, Jesus initiated his mother-in-law into the mystery of his resurrection so that she could become his follower. Later, Jesus expressly declared that the Sabbath was made for people, thus that rules must serve the people's well-being, and for this he ended up in conflicts that ultimately cost him his life.

To follow means to let go. We, too, stand today in tension between renewal and tradition, between charism and office. Both the Roman Catholic and the Orthodox Churches have a hard time letting go of traditional structures. This is understandable, considering that one is talking about a long tradition and does not want to break with it. Perhaps it may be helpful to revisit the house of Simon and Andrew, seeing the pope as successor of Peter and the patriarch of Constantinople as successor of Andrew. Could they not, like the two brothers, let themselves be taught afresh by Jesus, with Simon's mother-in-law as a model, what it means to be grasped by him? Is it not a matter of letting go of the nets of the past, which sometimes hold one captive, to follow in Jesus's footsteps?

For several decades, women have been ordained for various ministries in the churches that emerged from the Reformation. It appears obvious that most of the Catholic faithful accept them as clergy of equal value. That, too, is worthy of consideration. Perhaps these churches demonstrate better examples of discipleship regarding the question of women clergy, since they, like Jesus, raise up women and admit them to the ministry and, with them as examples, show a way forward to the churches that appeal to the authority of Peter and Andrew.

In any case, Jesus has recognized the plight of women and has clearly accepted the service of a woman in Simon and Andrew's house. He wanted to have an example. With Simon's mother-in-law, women's service in the church is briefly and succinctly written for us in our foundational text. The women, in any case, can't be blamed that they are lying in bed with a fever—nor can we men. But we could make some changes if we take the "fisher of people" from Nazareth as our model. Can we really justify dispensing with women's charisms by giving the house of Simon and Andrew a wide berth and leaving Capernaum? Considering its origins, wouldn't the church enhance its authenticity by ordaining women?

At any rate, Jesus later instructed his disciples one more time at the house in Capernaum. When it comes to service and devotion in his church, he doesn't give up.

Chapter 2

A WOMAN REVEALS HER SECRET

Some time ago I heard a lovely anecdote: At a party for her ninetieth birthday, one of the well-wishers asked the jubilarian how she had managed to reach such an advanced age without experiencing health limitations. The jubilarian replied, "Well, now I'll tell you my secret. Every day I eat a clove of garlic." Whereupon one of her grandchildren drily commented, "Grandma, that's no secret!"

I like that anecdote because it expresses something significant about the German word *Geheimnis*, which can mean "secret" or "mystery." This word *Geheimnis* was created by Martin Luther (1483–1546), who coined it for the Greek word *mysterion* or, rather, for the Latin word *sacramentum*, when he was translating the Bible into German. It contains the word *Heim*, which is associated with "familiar" and "at home." Someone who shares a secret with another is, as a rule, familiar with that person. So Goethe (1749–1832) was able to declare, "The one who confides the secret is already at home!"*

Of course, much secrecy or secretiveness is also associated with secrets. With many of our secrets, we're glad if they don't

* Translator's note: This is a play on words: "secret" = *Geheimnis*, "at home" = *daheim*.

come to light but remain hidden in our hearts. And yet we are also familiar with the experience of great relief when a secret is revealed and we're finally freed from its burden. To be sure, considerable sensibility and discretion are required so that no painful revelations come out into the open.

In our church the seal of confession is a great good. I am very thankful that I can discreetly confide my failures to a brother and do not need to confess my sins to the entire community, as was done in the early church. Even if my contrition remains in the hiddenness of the sacrament, after confession I experience a feeling of liberation or, as a young father expressed it so beautifully during an evening for first communicants' parents, "For me confession is like the spring! I feel new life!"

It requires some effort for me to describe my transgressions in words. I find many of them unpleasant, and they fill me with shame. But through the very process of my expressing them, evil thoughts and intentions that no one wants to know about lose their power over me. When I put them into words in confession, they no longer belong exclusively to me. They are emptied out of my innermost self and thereby cast out of my heart. This is precisely what St. Benedict means when he recommends, "As soon as wrongful thoughts come into your heart, dash them against Christ and disclose them to your spiritual father" (RB 4.50). What we keep in secret in our heart loses its power when we open our hearts, so that we can experience reconciliation and healing. Or we can also put it like this: many unpleasant secrets must be expressed in words so that we can be freed from them and thereby find ourselves again and be comfortable with ourselves once more.

This is what finally happens when I entrust myself to the mystery of God in the sacrament. God has created everything good and will bring everything to completion in his goodness. We Christians believe that God's mystery has been incarnated in Jesus of Nazareth—comprehensible and tangible, so that we can be made whole in our encounter with him. This was the experience of a seriously ill woman who surreptitiously touched Jesus and of the young girl whom he raised up. Both find their way home to themselves, because "the one who confides the secret is already at home."

THE SELF-ASSURED OUTCAST

When Jesus had crossed again in the boat to the other side, a great crowd gathered around him; and he was by the sea. Then one of the leaders of the synagogue named Jairus came and, when he saw him, fell at his feet and begged him repeatedly, "My little daughter is at the point of death. Come and lay your hands on her, so that she may be made well, and live." So he went with him.

And a large crowd followed him and pressed in on him. Now there was a woman who had been suffering from hemorrhages for twelve years. She had endured much under many physicians, and had spent all that she had; and she was no better, but rather grew worse. She had heard about Jesus, and came up behind him in the crowd and touched his cloak, for she said, "If I but touch his clothes, I will be made well." Immediately her hemorrhage stopped; and she felt in her body that she was healed of her disease. Immediately aware that power had gone forth from him, Jesus turned about in the crowd and said, "Who touched my clothes?" And his disciples said to him, "You see the crowd pressing in on you; how can you say, 'Who touched me?'" He looked all around to see who had done it. But the woman, knowing what had happened to her, came in fear and trembling, fell down before him, and told him the whole truth. He said to her, "Daughter, your faith

> has made you well; go in peace, and be healed of your disease."
>
> While he was still speaking, some people came from the leader's house to say, "Your daughter is dead. Why trouble the teacher any further?" But overhearing what they said, Jesus said to the leader of the synagogue, "Do not fear, only believe." He allowed no one to follow him except Peter, James, and John, the brother of James. When they came to the house of the leader of the synagogue, he saw a commotion, people weeping and wailing loudly. When he had entered, he said to them, "Why do you make a commotion and weep? The child is not dead but sleeping." And they laughed at him. Then he put them all outside, and took the child's father and mother and those who were with him, and went in where the child was. He took her by the hand and said to her, "Talitha cum," which means, "Little girl, get up!" And immediately the girl got up and began to walk about (she was twelve years of age). At this they were overcome with amazement. He strictly ordered them that no one should know this, and told them to give her something to eat. (Mark 5:21–43)

Even though we're going to consider the awakening of the daughter of Jairus in more detail in the next chapter, a few thoughts are in order here because both stories are artfully interwoven. One is the daughter of Jairus, the other is addressed by Jesus as "my daughter." One is twelve years old; the other has been ill for twelve years. In the eyes of their contemporaries, both would have been considered unclean and would have been isolated, one by death and the other by her flow of blood. And finally, both women were saved: The young girl was saved and remained alive! The sick woman was saved by her faith and received new vitality! Once again, then, we see that Jesus had no fear of touching women, whether unclean because of a hemorrhage or unclean because of death. Both stories provide an answer to the question raised earlier by the disciples: "Who then is this?" (Mark 4:41). He is the Savior who brings new life, so that God's nearness and splendor shine through him. Even the name Jairus indicates this because many exegetes translate it as "God will awaken!" "God will shine forth!" Both women experience this in their own bodies.

Before telling of these healings, Mark had described how Jesus had tamed a violent storm that seriously threatened the lives of the disciples in their boat. Awakened from his sleep, Jesus showed himself to be Lord over the forces of nature. The story contains a deep testimony to faith. He is the Risen One who has unlimited power, even over death itself! This alone is the message of the two women's Easter stories: Jesus saves from death, whether it be the social death of exclusion or the real death at the end of life!

After quieting the storm, Jesus healed a man who was possessed by an unclean spirit and, separated from his family, was living among the tombs. This took place in the country of the Gerasenes, on the eastern shore of the lake (see Mark 5:1–20). Figuratively speaking, we could say that Jesus freed a person from the isolation of the tomb and brought him back from death to life, so that he found his way home to his family. This theme also shines through the two healings that follow: In that Jesus heals the unclean woman and calls her "daughter," she finds her way back to God's family. Similarly, the dead young girl is given back to her family as a living person! The one who confides the secret is already at home!

Let us look more closely at the healing of the woman with the hemorrhage. After his trip to the eastern shore of the lake, Jesus now returns to the western shore. There an unimaginable crowd of people gathers; each of them wants to see up close this wonderworker from Nazareth, whose reputation must have spread through Galilee like wildfire.

In this crowd is a woman who has suffered from a hemorrhage for twelve years—a long time. According to the law of Moses she is chronically unclean, and everything she touches automatically becomes unclean (see Lev 15:19). She is completely excluded from social and cultic life. She may not allow a child to sit on her lap, may not embrace a friend, may not embrace a man, may not take part in a feast, and so forth. Ultimately, she is condemned to a social death because of her disorder.

A hemorrhage means that she is continuously losing vitality. For twelve years she has probably been occupied exclusively with this one theme: "My sickness and I!" She has already tried everything possible. She has spent a lot of money on doctors, but nothing has helped her, so her illness has also led her gradually into financial ruin. Considered matter-of-factly, she finds herself in a hopeless and demoralizing predicament and is probably close to giving up.

"She had heard about Jesus," Mark says succinctly (5:27), and now she tries everything to meet this wonderworker. This is a significant statement about faith. Faith comes from hearing and needs us to do our part! The sick woman doesn't wallow in self-pity; she acts independently; indeed, she actively takes her life into her own hands. "If I but touch his clothes, I will be made well" (Mark 5:28). Supporting this is the faith that Jesus must be utterly filled with divine power, so that simply the contact with his garment suffices for her to be healed! That is a faith that confers health, that heals.

Protected by the hiddenness and anonymity of the crowd, the unclean woman secretly pushes forward toward Jesus. After all, no one must notice that she wants to touch Jesus, because doing so would violate the law; she would incur punishment because Jesus, too, would be made unclean through contact with her. But her faith that she would be healed is obviously greater than her fear of breaking the law. In secrecy she exceeds the limits of what is permitted and experiences the impossible: She feels in her body "that she was healed of her disease" (Mark 5:29). That is an awakening to new life. That is Easter. She experiences the nearness of God's kingdom up close in her own body!

It is striking that until this moment Jesus remains silent. But now he asks the disciples a question they don't understand: "Who touched me?" Even we wouldn't understand his reaction if we hadn't had the background information that Jesus felt the power going out from him. The frank question and the way Jesus looks out into the crowd startle the woman so that in fear and trembling she emerges from the secrecy granted by hiding in the anonymous mass of people. Anyone who has been caught and exposed before everyone can well sympathize with how she must have felt.

As a sign of reverence, she falls down in front of Jesus and confesses everything to him—the whole truth. In so doing, she reveals her secret. In this context it is very instructive to go back to the original meaning of the Greek word for "truth"—*aletheia*. It comes from *alethos* and means "not hidden," "unconcealed." Thus the woman emerges from her hiddenness and thereby becomes the preacher of unconcealed, visible faith. This is precisely what Jesus wants to point out when he openly asks after her. He's interested not in exposing her but in affirming her witness to her faith! Those who are present are meant to learn from this woman to have faith. Jesus neither rebukes her nor says anything about how he experienced power going out from him. He puts the woman, not himself, in the center and thus praises her action, affirming her in front of everyone: "Daughter, your faith has made you well; go in peace, and be healed of your disease" (Mark 5:34). When one considers that women, as already mentioned, were not allowed to proclaim their faith openly in the Jewish community, then this statement is a provocation and refers forward to the women on Easter morning. The woman who has been healed becomes, through Jesus, a preacher of truth—of visible faith. She is no longer excluded from society. Jesus underlines this when he addresses her as "daughter." As a beloved child, she belongs once again to God's family and thus to the chosen people as well. Here the address "daughter" recalls Jesus's conflict with his own family, who wish to bring him back from public life to Nazareth, back to the hiddenness of the home. But Jesus resists and states, "Whoever does the will of God is my brother and sister and mother" (Mark 3:35).

That is the deeper meaning behind this story of awakening. Easter means to do God's will and, like this woman, to act contrary to all life-threatening structures. Easter means encountering the One who has so much life energy that he breaks through isolation and conquers death, so that he can say, "My child, your faith has saved you. Go in peace! You are freed from your suffering!"

The healing of the unclean woman demonstrates to the reader that Jesus wants to free people into life. Faith in him should not force one into secrets. Indeed, Jesus motivates us to step out of our seclusion and to speak the truth. This is how liberation happens.

The faith path that this woman has traveled, determinedly and on her own initiative, leaves a lasting impression. As a model she motivates us not to resign ourselves to limitations but to break courageously with rules that stand in the way of healing. The woman represents a faith that heals, and she can strengthen us to take our life bravely in our hands according to the axiom, "The one who confides the secret is already home!"

MORE CREDIBILITY BY ABOLISHING MANDATORY CELIBACY?

The fate of the healed woman reminds me of a woman's anonymous account that I once read in a large German daily newspaper. For many years, she writes, she has been the female companion of a Catholic priest whom she loves very much. As with many similar relationships, this one is a complete secret. She writes that she well understands why her companion cannot give up his vocation. Ultimately, he has followed his calling and wants to serve the gospel. Her love came along later. Nor does she want to pressure him further because she knows that his work gives him purpose and fulfillment and how much his parishioners need and appreciate him as their pastor. And yet she would gladly cast off this secrecy, stand at his side as his wife, hug him openly, hold his hand, and enjoy esteem and social recognition as his partner. Thus, they are forced always to take care never to be seen together in public or to be too familiar with each other. How lovely it would be, she continues, if they could have had children together. But now it is too late for that. And what will happen when they get old or sick?

The honesty of this account, which was written without bitterness, affected me deeply, and this woman's situation reminded me of the fate of the woman in the Gospel, who, condemned to social death, was summoned by Jesus out of the hiddenness of her life. Secret friendships with Catholic priests are a painful chapter in the history of the Catholic Church. The celibate life is certainly a high good. It ensures openness and availability for God's work, and we priests have made a free decision to live such a life. It also involves being able to tolerate being alone. Sadly, however, not everyone is capable of this, so that many men have relinquished their priestly or monastic vocations. Many of them found happiness in a partnership and no longer grieve for their priestly calling. Others are hurt that they still feel themselves called but are not allowed to serve anymore. But this is only the men's perspective.

Women who must go along with such a decision are equally affected by it. They, too, spend part of their life in secrecy. When I read this article, I thought of women I know who have gone lovingly and faithfully through life as companions to men who were priests. Surely, at the beginning, as in every love, there was the yearning for tenderness, strong sexual desire, and the desire to become one with another. All of that is, indeed, fulfilling and a gift of God. But with the passing of years, something still deeper matures. I think of a priest, now deceased, who during a difficult life crisis at the age of fifty fell in love with a woman and remained in a relationship with her until he died. They had lived together for a long time but then realized that, on account of their different conditioning, such an intense life partnership was not possible. That wasn't easy for either of them to accept. For a lifetime they struggled together. His partner had shared in all his personal and vocational highs and lows, and indeed out of love even advised him not to give up his priestly ministry. He could easily have lived on her income or entered the teaching profession, but she simply knew how much he was molded by his vocation. This was his life's work! When he became seriously ill, it was his female companion who faithfully cared for him, devotedly looked after him, and was there for him with her loving presence when he died. He was a good pastor who was highly appreciated for his humanness. He very probably credited his female companion for his sensitivity toward people because she occasionally brought him down to earth so that he didn't become pompous, as he said of himself.

Frequently it is strong, self-confident women who enter relationships with priests. A Protestant pastor who had leadership responsibility in his regional church once said to me, "Imagine the good that such couples could accomplish in your church!" Regarding the pastoral needs caused by the so-called lack of priests, this provides food for thought. It is good that mandatory celibacy is currently a controversial topic of discussion in our church. But this should not happen only in the context of an emergency that has resulted in the consideration of possibly ordaining married men or reactivating priests who have left to get married, solely for the purpose of alleviating the lack of priests. This has merit, to be sure, but in the end, mandatory celibacy, with its disadvantages, is a matter of reversing a need. What need for secrecy could be reversed if men had the option of serving as priests either alone or with a woman at their side? This is a matter of honesty and genuineness and of the desire at last to be able to leave a clandestine life behind. The church would profit from truthfulness and credibility. Imagine the benefits to be had from an honest opening of the heart! For the church, too, it would be a relief that ultimately could bring about healing and recovery. Many women and men would be liberated from their guilty consciences and their secretiveness and could then, like the woman who was healed in the Gospel, freely take their places in the life of the church community.

In this context, yet another ecclesial topic comes to mind: how we handle couples whose first marriage has broken and who seek a new beginning. Jesus indisputably warned about the arbitrariness of adultery (see Mark 10:1–12). Marriage, as sacrament, is a precious good that makes visible the mystery of God's love. One does not play around with love, and sometimes it seems that many couples are very quick to separate from each other without first trying to work out their issues and think about their future together. But earlier, when separation was a social taboo, was everything really better, as one sometimes hears? Look at how much deceit this attitude brought in its wake! How, especially, must the women have suffered whose husbands were living secretly in another relationship, or who were subject to domestic violence by their dissatisfied husbands! How many couples remained together to maintain a good appearance to the outside world when a separation was out of the question! Behind closed doors, many of them made their lives hell for each other.

From the perspective of canon law, a judgment after a divorce is simple. A second marriage does not exist, and the same argument could be raised as with celibacy: the concerned parties should have considered earlier the consequences of a church marriage. But this doesn't consider the realities of life, in which not everything can be planned according to what one would have liked. There are genuine cases of growing alienation that can and must lead to painful separations. Why, then, can there be no second chance? This is surely something that Jesus never intended when he especially wanted to protect women from being divorced by their husbands on any old grounds that the latter chose (see Mark 10:1–12). Jesus speaks quite clearly about adultery in which a man dismisses his wife, or a wife dismisses her husband and remarries. But the history of God with humanity is full of rifts, and despite this, God again and again has risked beginning anew with his people. Precisely because of this, God has come near to us humans in the person of his Son, in order to tear down borders and with his life force to make all things new. The woman in the Gospel experienced this when she touched his garment and thereby courageously broke with the religious precepts of her time. Right up to our own time she proclaims the belief that closeness to Jesus frees one from isolation, removes a scourge, and confers a new perspective on life.

This, however, has consequences for the oft-discussed question of the reception of communion by divorced and remarried Catholics. If Jesus is truly present with his Body and Blood in bread and wine, as we believe and confess in the sacrament of the Eucharist, then that can only motivate one to touch his garment and to receive him in the form of bread and wine. The uncleanness of the woman in the Gospel didn't harm him, quite the opposite: she experienced healing! And so he cannot be harmed by serious sin. As if we could infect or defile him! Rather, it is important to have confidence in the healing power of the sacrament of reconciliation and of the Eucharist, to seek God's healing nearness there like the woman did, so that humans in their brokenness can hear the words of beginning anew: "My daughter, my son, your faith has saved you. Go in peace! You are healed of your suffering." In any case, for this woman the corner of his garment sufficed for her to be completely healed! She did not resign herself to the laws but took her own fate into her hands. Jesus exposed her courageous deed in front of everyone: "Your faith has saved you!" Her faith made her whole because the one who confides the secret is already at home.

Chapter 3

A WOMAN RETURNS TO LIFE

I delight in watching children when they unwrap presents and enjoy their new toys. On one of those occasions, a child asked me what my favorite toy was. At the time I couldn't give an answer, and, on reflection, I realized that something essential is missing in our lives if we have nothing to play with.

Play is, on the one hand, purposeless, but on the other hand, is not without meaning. It relaxes us, takes us out of ourselves, and pulls us out of life's seriousness. Play promotes our creativity and spontaneity. In play we show our true face; for example, if we cannot lose or we rejoice in overtaking a fellow player to be first in reaching the goal.

Theologian Hugo Rahner (1900–1968) writes that we, as humans, are images of the "playful God" (Latin *deus ludens*). All of creation should be an expression of God's playful creativity. Understood this way, it's a delightful idea to awaken the child in us in order thereby to playfully experience life from another perspective. What childhood images appear in my mind? What has become of them? What are the dreams of my youth? What were or are my favorite playthings?

All of this helps us to remain open to new things and protects us from continually complaining about how bad the world is or lamenting everything that is no more. It also motivates us to continue to live more playfully and to ask ourselves, What will God surprise us with today? Where in church and society is he awakening new life, and what can we learn from this? How will he lure us out of our comfort zones so that we discover new possibilities for play?

In this context it can help to consider children and young people. They explore their world step by step. They also experiment with risking failure. Children are still able to trust. They are open and vulnerable and freely show their affections. Young people have dreams and visions, rich fantasies, and believe in ideals for a better world.

Many of the challenges and problems of our time would lose something of their gravity if we approached them with a youthful lightness. Even our church could benefit from a bit more *joie de vivre*—more delight in life.

In our *Rule*, St. Benedict recommends that the abbot ask the advice of the younger members of the monastery because "the Lord often reveals what is better to the younger" (RB 3.3). For one thing, beginners still have ideals and are closer to the source of their vocation. For example, they still arrive punctually for worship services, take joy in wearing the habit in public, or take the time to listen again to many familiar stories from an older brother. One can often learn from the novices how the monastic ideal appears. Not only that, they also bring innovative ideas and will question routines: Why do you do it this way? What history and what beliefs are behind this tradition? Could this not be done differently? I have an idea about this, and so on.

All of this resonates when Jesus, in the Gospel story about the dead girl, says, "The child is not dead, she is just sleeping!"

THE DAUGHTER RETURNED TO LIFE

> While he was still speaking, some people came from the leader's house to say, "Your daughter is dead. Why trouble the teacher any further?" But overhearing what they said, Jesus said to the leader of the synagogue, "Do not fear, only believe." He allowed no one to follow him except Peter, James, and John, the brother of James. When they came to the house of the leader of the synagogue, he saw a commotion, people weeping and wailing loudly. When he had entered, he said to them, "Why do you make a commotion and weep? The child is not dead but sleeping." And they laughed at him. Then he put them all outside, and took the child's father and mother and those who were with him, and went in where the child was. He took her by the hand and said to her, "Talitha cum," which means, "Little girl, get up!" And immediately the girl got up and began to walk about (she was twelve years of age). At this they were overcome with amazement. He strictly ordered them that no one should know this, and told them to give her something to eat. (Mark 5:35–43)

Mark's Gospel reports only one instance of a raising from the dead, and this involves a young woman. In the other Gospels men, too, are awakened to new life (see Luke 7:11–17; John 11:11–44). Thus this most spectacular miracle of Mark's Gospel corresponds with the healing of Simon's mother-in-law at the beginning as well as with Jesus's resurrection at the end, which is announced to the three women at the tomb. One could almost think that resurrection and Easter pertain first of all to women. At the same time, it is the child's father, Jairus, who very confidently begs Jesus to heal his daughter. He wants Jesus to come to his house, touch his daughter, and thereby save her and bring her life. And Jesus goes with him. This circumstance alone is already "good news"—*evangelium*—for Jairus and for us readers. Jesus accompanies us humans. He shares our pain and lets himself be moved by our prayers. He brings salvation and life!

A depressing drama lies in the intertwining of the two stories of healing: While the woman who suffers from a hemorrhage receives new life as "daughter" through Jesus, at the same time the father is given the sad news: "Your daughter has died!" One would almost think that the delay caused by the healing of one woman has led to the death of the other. But Jesus tells Jairus, "Don't be afraid, just have faith!" Thus the woman who has been healed becomes an example for the synagogue official. Just as she was helped by her faith, so, too, Jairus's plea will not go unheard. At the same time, the disciples, hearing Jesus say, "Do not fear, only believe," recall their doubt during the storm at sea, when Jesus chided them, "Why are you afraid? Have you still no faith?" (Mark 4:40). The gist of this saying of Jesus is that fear is always the opposite of trust because fear constricts us and inhibits our life.

Jesus's choice of Peter, James, and John as his three companions indicates that something exclusive is about to happen. Later, Jesus will climb the mountain of the transfiguration with them. There it will be demonstrated to them that Jesus of Nazareth is God's Son, who will overcome death (see Mark 9:2–8). Later, the night before Jesus dies, these three will fall asleep on the Mount of Olives (see Mark 14:32–42). Three times he has to wake them up! The two scenes correspond with the story of the raising of Jairus's daughter, when Jesus says of her, "She is only sleeping!" In contrast to the three courageous women who accompany Jesus on his ordeal all the way to the cross and visit his grave on Easter morning, the disciples fail. All they really would have needed to do was to recall what they experienced in Jairus's house and on the mount of transfiguration. Instead, overcome with fear and anxiety, they fly the coop. Mark doesn't wish to use this story to criticize their shameful behavior. Rather, he uses it to present the disciples as comfort and encouragement for the oppressed community that suffers from contempt and persecution as well as for each reader whose faith is attacked and who feels anxious. Even when we fail, we can nonetheless hope for a new beginning. Again and again. God sparks new life into being.

But let's return to the raising of Jairus's daughter. This event, like the healing of Simon's mother-in-law, takes place within the privacy of a house. By visiting the house of Jairus, Jesus enters the realm of death! He faces concrete human misery, even our experiences of death!

While the mourners freely express their sorrow by weeping and sobbing, Jesus does not accept this view of death. With an air of authority, he throws out of the house everyone who claims the girl is dead. Here Mark uses the Greek word *ekbalo*, which appears in connection with the driving out of demons (see Mark 1:34) as well as in the cleansing of the temple, when Jesus drives the merchants and money-changers out of God's house, saying that the house of God may not be turned into a den of thieves (see Mark 11:15–17). The same is true of the house of Jairus. There is no room for sorrow and mourning in the place in which someone is to be raised from the dead: "The child is not dead but sleeping" (Mark 5:39). The evangelist makes a profound point here. In the sight of God, death is only sleep from which he will awaken the deceased. This means that death is only temporary.

The comment about the sleeping child corresponds to the miracle of the stilling of the storm on the lake about which Mark had written earlier. In this crisis, the disciples awaken the sleeping Jesus with the reproach, "Teacher, do you not care that we are perishing?" (Mark 4:38). Roused from sleep, Jesus now commands the forces of nature so that the disciples will not perish in the nighttime storm but will be saved from it. He is the fisher of people! The experience of the young girl whom Jesus awakens from sleep is no different—as we might also say, she has been "fished" from the night of death into new life.

The raising of the girl thereby recalls the healing of Simon's mother-in-law: Jesus grasps the young girl by the hand. Here, too, the Greek word *krateo* is used. By touching the girl, Jesus gives her new vitality. He initiates her into his life principle, into the paschal mystery, so that her father's wish for her salvation and life is fulfilled. Once again Jesus has no fear of being made unclean by physical contact, in this case with a dead person. He addresses her authoritatively: "Wake up! Stand up!" That is the voice of one who awakens people from the dead. Again Mark uses the word *egeirein*—"to awaken." In the house of Jairus Easter is made a reality!

The story of the twelve-year-old girl concerns someone on the verge of being a teenager. She is no longer only a child, nor is she an adult; thus she symbolizes the future. When Jesus commands her to walk around and asks those present to give her something to eat, it's clear that the young woman is truly alive, she has only been sleeping! The place of mourning is now filled with new life. There is something light and playful about the closing scene. It's as if the deadly serious mood is blown away and youthful vitality spreads.

This spectacular raising from the dead could surely not be kept a secret. Jesus's plea for silence means, rather, that the raising of the twelve-year-old girl can first truly be understood only in the context of his death and resurrection (see Mark 16:6).

Basically, the raising of Jairus's daughter carries the message that Jesus has declared victory over all life-destroying powers, including death! He doesn't resign himself to death but has power over it. This has consequences for our faith: Jesus wants us to have life. Or as he expresses it: God is a God of the living and not of the dead (see Mark 12:27). He breaches the laws of birth and decay. What this means for the communities of disciples throughout time, however, is that we must prepare, not for death, but for life with Jesus. Whoever is, like Jairus's daughter, grasped by him has life and will be surprised by life over and over. "Little girl, I say to you, stand up!" That is the Easter message that the girl wordlessly proclaims by standing up and filling the house with life.

INCREASED VIGOR BY ALLOWING YOUNG PEOPLE TO EXPERIMENT?

Many active Christians in the United States and Europe are concerned about the future of the church. Constantly high numbers of people leaving the church, the evaporation of the practice and knowledge of the faith, the decline in full-time and voluntary workers, the closing of churches, and many other things describe the dramatic downward trend of recent decades. Much about church life has met its demise, and the mood in the parishes is characterized more by sad resignation than by joyful optimism. Where will all this lead?

To be sure, the upheaval that we have been experiencing now for several decades is serious and demands that we let go of much that was once built up with great dedication. This grieving process is difficult for everyone involved, when, for example, parishes lose the autonomy that they had once won, then churches and parish centers that were once established at great cost must be demolished or religious houses rich in tradition closed. Everywhere these situations are lamented, on the one hand, with the expectation that perhaps something could still be changed, and on the other, with the conviction that much worse is yet to come. But then don't we resemble the mourners who lamented the premature death of Jairus's daughter?

In contrast is the faith of Jairus, who begs for salvation and life for his child. We could ask, along with him, What child lies dying today in our house, in our church, for whom we beg for life and salvation?

STAND UP!

We pray a great deal for the future of the church. We pray for more vocations to the priesthood and the religious life. We pray that the faith will spread and will blossom to new life in the coming generations. This assurance in prayer is certainly an asset, for which we may be thankful. But do we allow Jesus to really awaken new life or aren't we sometimes like the messengers of death who convey the sad news: "Your daughter is dead. Why bother the Teacher further?" How often do I hear, "But that makes no sense! The era of the church is past! Christianity in the West has served its purpose!" This assessment may be partially true, and perhaps it's even good if much of the past is consigned to the tomb.

In contrast, Jesus invites the girl to stand up and move, and he asks her parents to give their daughter something to eat. There, too, we can see ourselves: What "food," in the figurative sense, can we offer young people today? What ecclesiastical leeway or experimentation and playing fields do we open up to them? Can we believe that God sometimes reveals through the disciples what is the better thing?

It is understandable that traditional beliefs and ideas on morality don't mean much to many young people. To be sure, there are well-meaning attempts at intervention, such as the *YOUCAT* (Youth Catechism of the Catholic Church) or youth churches. But these methods only seldom reach young people who have distanced themselves from the church. It would be an exciting project to assume responsibility for these things in a playful manner. For example, as teachers of the faith, what would they make of the Virgin Birth or the primacy of the pope? What decisions would they make if, as bishop of a diocese, they were confronted with the lack of priests? How would they assess homosexuality or artificial contraception or other topics?

Considering the present-day challenges we face, we are justified in asking, When do we really listen to children and youth and take their advice seriously? I feel, especially at confirmations, how the church is brimming with vitality through the young people. How lovely it would be if it stayed this way. Certainly this would mean allowing changes or even giving up many a cherished tradition. How much leeway do we have?

In this context I recall a bishop's homily I heard on the Feast of the Assumption. "It is remarkable that the Bible contains absolutely nothing specific about this feast," the bishop said, and he went on to compare the church with a man who had gotten married in his younger years. With each new year of married life, he would discover new aspects of his wife, so that only over the course of a lifetime was he able to come to know her full personality. I liked this comparison because it describes a process of development of the faith and leaves much open for the future. Can it thus be that new worlds of faith will be opened up to us precisely through young people? In looking back at the long evolution of the church's faith, can there take place a new consideration of which topics are of existential importance for Christianity and which are less so? Could even the ecumenical process thereby acquire new vitality?

In my encounters with young people I am repeatedly surprised by their uncomplicated approach to many a problem that for us adults appears almost insoluble. It would be an experiment once again openly to trust Jesus and his words: "Why do you make a commotion and weep? The child is not dead but sleeping!" Can we permit Jesus to wake up his church by calling to us, "Little girl, I say to you, stand up!"? Here it would be equally exciting to discover what new faith movements exist in the so-called young churches of Africa or Asia. I am impressed again and again how naïvely and openheartedly Christians on these continents speak about Jesus and his presence in their lives and what great confidence in God they have. The same is true of the so-called neophytes among us. Sometimes it may seem somewhat strange at first when people speak so straightforwardly about God's existence and Jesus as ever-present. That can naturally get on one's nerves. At the same time, however, it is a challenge: How do you speak about him, how do you bring him into the conversation? What does it mean for us as church and as parishes when we become smaller and lose power? Is that approximately what is meant when Jesus invites us to become like children?

Perhaps this process of becoming smaller is really a great chance to awaken the child anew by exploring other, perhaps even strange-seeming ways of proclaiming the faith. In this connection I think of a group of young people whom I encountered during a workshop on youth mission at a Catholic youth festival. At first, I thought that the discussion was about how today's youth could be missionized. Soon, however, I realized differently. A young man told the participants that he had resumed going to church a while ago. In the course of this, the gospel about the sending forth of the disciples that comes after the story of the raising of Jairus's daughter in Mark's Gospel was proclaimed (see Mark 6:6–12). Earlier Jesus had experienced rejection in his own family and his hometown, and consequently he set out for the neighboring villages. Here he sent out his disciples two by two with the instruction to take nothing along with them—no bread, no sack, and so on. The young man at the workshop commented, "Cool, I want to try that too!" And so he sought like-minded companions. They agreed ahead of time what could and could not be taken along: no money, no cellphones, only the most necessary articles of clothing and other things. They started out on the morning of Pentecost Monday and first spent some time at a lake, since the weather was nice. But at some point, they began feeling hungry and thirsty. So they set out for the nearest village, rang the doorbells of the houses, and offered their services: "Can we mow your lawn or wash your car?" They were asked, "For what do you need the money?" Their stereotypical answer was, "We take the gospel seriously." Then they spoke about their project, with the result that soon they were invited to dinner and found a place to stay for the night! The next day they walked through the countryside and passed by a woman farmer who was working in her garden. Somewhat curious, she wanted to know whether they were a hiking group. They replied, "No, we take the gospel seriously!" Once again they were invited in. In the evening they helped out in the barn, heard the widow's life and faith story, and exchanged views with her. The next day they stopped at a train station, unpacked their guitars, played music, and set a hat out in front of them. "What are you collecting for?" asked the people who were waiting for trains. Again they answered, "We take the gospel seriously!" and told their story. This story of the "youth mission" made a lasting impression on me. How would confirmation preparation in our parishes look if the candidates were sent out like this for one day along with older youths? Could that not also be a project for, say, a newly elected parish council? How would a cathedral chapter fare if their inner child were to be awakened in this way? Perhaps we should really take the gospel seriously in a more naïve way and cultivate pleasure in bringing the good news into conversation and among the people with a little more playfulness.

In any case, one thing is clear: Neither the messengers of death nor the women mourners have any place in the house of Jairus. They have death in them. Jesus, in contrast, awakens the child, just as did saints such as Francis (1181–1226), Philip Neri (1515–95), Don Bosco (1815–88), and many others who later emulated him. For example, Francis, with childlike confidence in God, preached to the animals and reenacted the nativity scene with his contemporaries. Many humorous anecdotes about Philip Neri have come down to us, and Don Bosco opened himself completely to the world of children and young people. All these saints stand for the playfulness of being and trusted in this saying: "Whoever does not receive the kingdom of God as a little child will never enter it" (Mark 10:15).

Perhaps we are really much too grown-up when we rationally object, "That can't be done! We've always done it this way! That's our tradition!" These are actually so-called killer arguments that destroy new life. In so doing we sometimes resemble parents who don't want to understand that their children will gradually grow up, go their own ways, little by little accept responsibility, and must independently shape their lives. We want, above all, to protect them and enclose them in an ivory tower of faith certainties and moral views.

The raising of the daughter of Jairus is a motivation not only to give young people in our church room to live and to play, to call to them, "Stand up!" but also to awaken our inner child.

In this context we must be aware that teenagers don't do everything right, and many experiences during puberty are bitter and indeed can hurt and disillusion. Even this girl and her parents were not spared that. Young people need freedom to experience things for themselves. Yet, they still need correction by adults. Admittedly, it is often not at all simple to determine when a boundary should be set and when a long leash is required. Couldn't awakened teenagers, even when they are already in their late teens, help us once again to consider what is truly essential in our faith?

The Easter story that takes place in the house of Jairus encourages us to awaken our inner child. What sorts of things would take place in my life if I only had the courage! A therapist friend uses a beautiful image for this. She says that two children live in her soul. One is a youth who is very prudent and reasonable. His severe gray clothing slightly resembles that of a monk. He leaves nothing to chance. He wants to plan everything in detail and to organize it judiciously. The other child is a chubby girl with a fiery red dress who simply wants to enjoy life. Her vitality can scarcely be contained, and she tries out many new things. She is repeatedly reprimanded by the boy. But sometimes, when he is asleep or not watching, this girl encourages the therapist to try crazy things or to give her emotions free rein. Both children are important for her, so she can't afford to neglect any part of either of them in her life. Occasionally they fight with each other, and sometimes the boy wins, sometimes the girl....

This image speaks to me. It might do all of us "men of the church" good to give the chubby girl with her fiery red dress more leeway, completely in accord with Jesus's invitation: "Talitha cum—little girl, I say to you, stand up!"

Chapter 4

A WOMAN CORRECTS THE TEACHER

Healthy self-awareness is worth a lot. It testifies to identity, assertiveness, and self-confidence. Of course, it can also lead to unfortunate pride and blind egocentrism that accepts nothing as valid other than oneself.

It happens repeatedly that exclusive claims slip into forms of extremism that, in turn, result in national and religious fundamentalism. Then people, nationalities, and religions no longer encounter one another respectfully on an equal footing but pursue their exclusive claims to salvation about which they find it necessary to persuade their opposite numbers—in serious cases, even with force. Germany's painful history of Nazism and the Holocaust, as well as many an inglorious development in church history, such as the persecution of heretics or the Jewish pogroms, illustrate the inhuman systems to which fundamentalisms can lead.

With a view to religious or nationalistic tendencies that have newly arisen in recent years, it is necessary to counteract at an early stage the dangerous consequences of such narrowmindedness.

These challenges recall the hospitality that St. Benedict asks us monks to take to heart (see RB 53). Hospitality is never one-sided and can even result in delightful experiences for the host that serve his or her own renewal. Nevertheless, conflicts and disappointments are not categorically excluded.

Benedict makes this clear when he writes in the chapter on the reception of visiting monks, "He [the visitor] may, indeed, with all humility and love make some reasonable criticisms or observations, which the abbot should prudently consider; it is possible that the Lord guided him to the monastery for this very purpose" (RB 61.4). It is interesting that here, as in other places in the *Rule*, Benedict uses the term *rationabiliter*—"prudently." It's precisely when uncomfortable things are appropriately and comprehensibly expressed by a guest that hospitality practiced can become an opportunity to be open to new perspectives and expand one's own horizons.

This is what Jesus experiences in his encounter with a foreign woman who simply makes her way into a house and asks him to heal her daughter.

THE ARTICULATE FOREIGNER

> From there he set out and went away to the region of Tyre. He entered a house and did not want anyone to know he was there. Yet he could not escape notice, but a woman whose little daughter had an unclean spirit immediately heard about him, and she came and bowed down at his feet. Now the woman was a Gentile, of Syrophoenician origin. She begged him to cast the demon out of her daughter. He said to her, "Let the children be fed first, for it is not fair to take the children's food and throw it to the dogs." But she answered him, "Sir, even the dogs under the table eat the children's crumbs." Then he said to her, "For saying that, you may go—the demon has left your daughter." So

> she went home, found the child lying on the bed, and the demon gone. (Mark 7:24–30)

This story is unique to Mark's Gospel. Only in this scene does Jesus deviate from his original conviction and allow himself to be taught. To be sure, he repeatedly disputes with the leading men of his time, but it is only in the conversation with this woman that a "course correction" occurs. Not just any woman, but a foreigner who doesn't even belong to the people of Israel corrects Jesus, so that he is presented to the reader as the one who is learning. In this connection the context of the encounter is interesting.

After Jesus had disputed vehemently about uncleanness with the Jewish religious authorities, he left his home in Galilee and traveled to the nearby foreign territories. During the dispute he had decisively pointed out that food from outside does not make a person unclean, as the Mosaic Law's precepts regarding purification prescribed (see Mark 7:1–23). Rather, it is solely evil thoughts, such as theft or murder, that arise within us that make people unclean. Only that would result in separation from God—that is, expressed theologically, in sin. Thus Jesus had seriously questioned the Jewish purification laws, as he had already done by healing the woman with the hemorrhage. Once again, the conflict with the scribes and Pharisees intensifies.

And so now Jesus travels to the foreign territory to the north, in the region of Tyre. As so often happens in border regions, here Jewish religion and culture mingled with other faiths. One could almost suspect that, after the dispute in his home territory, Jesus wanted to escape the narrowmindedness of his ancestral religion for a while.

Once again, Jesus retires to the security of a house. As with the healing of Simon's mother-in-law and the raising of Jairus's daughter, the reader is referred to something essential about his message. A woman from the neighborhood brazenly breaks into the privacy of the house and asks the foreign miracle worker to free her daughter from demonic powers. As if following the example of her predecessor, the woman with the hemorrhage, she oversteps the boundaries of decency. For one thing, a woman was not allowed simply to enter a strange house. For another, to a pious Jew it must have been an affront when a pagan woman came right up to him. This is again a matter of purity and impurity. But possibly the Syro-Phoenician woman knew nothing about the Judaic law.

In her anxiety about her daughter she comes straight to the point, falls down before Jesus as a sign of reverence, and begs him to heal her child. Why shouldn't her family, too, benefit from his healing power?

At first Jesus reacts dismissively to this intrusion into his private sphere. He curtly points out to the anxious mother that his mission focuses exclusively on the people of Israel, and he uses a very daring image by comparing the pagan peoples to dogs. Despite the deep conviction that Israel is God's chosen nation and despite all the love of spontaneity—sometimes indeed something just slips out of one's mouth—today such a comparison would justifiably bring vehement protests in its wake!

Even more astonishing is the woman's reaction. Without emotion she takes up his line of reasoning. She cleverly parries his belittling comparison. "Sir," she says, "even the dogs under the table eat the children's crumbs" (Mark 7:28). This quick-witted answer is simply genius. She turns a temporal "in succession"—"First the children, then the dogs!"—into a temporal "side-by-side"—"Children and dogs eat at the same time, the one at the table, the other under it." In so doing, the woman makes clear that both—children and dogs—have their place in the household, and the dogs are not banished from the house. In a figurative sense this means that for both, for Jews and pagans, there is sufficient nourishment in God's house because his goodness knows no limits. She addresses all people. Certainly Israel is the chosen people. But all other peoples also have their place in God's heart—this is the credo of this self-aware stranger.

Her argument also recalls the two multiplications of loaves that Mark's Gospel recounts that frame this scene, as it were (see Mark 6:35–44; 8:1–10). Jesus magnanimously provided first five thousand and then four thousand people with bread and fish, so that first twelve and then seven baskets, respectively, were left over. When people are prepared to share the little they have with one another, then there is enough for everyone, so goes the moral of these two stories of multiplication! Had Jesus perhaps forgotten this?

In any case, this courageous mother with her eloquence in no way resembles a puppy under the table. For Jesus she is much more an eye-level debate partner in whom he has met his match. At the same time, she preserves her style. She respectfully addresses Jesus as "Sir." This, too, is unique in Mark's Gospel and comes close to being a confession. When one considers that the title *Lord* (or "Sir") was only for God in Jewish usage, then it becomes clear that for this woman Jesus was more than an ordinary person. As with Peter, who shortly thereafter will observe, "You are the Messiah" (Mark 8:29), and as with the Roman centurion who recognizes the Son of God in the Crucified One (see Mark 15:39), so, too, for this woman the foreign miracle worker is "Sir"—a Lord! In contrast to the religious leaders of his own people who reject him, this foreign woman unknowingly becomes for the reader a witness of the Risen One! He is Lord over salvation and disaster, over life and death.

But that's not all. "You are right!" Jesus declares, and goes along with her line of reasoning: "For saying that, you may go—the demon has left your daughter" (Mark 7:29). Thus Jesus does not praise her faith, as he had done earlier with the woman with the hemorrhage. He explicitly praises her words, her reason and wisdom, as the Greek word *logos* indicates. Jesus lifts up her persistence in the discourse and her compelling reasoning as exemplary! Through this mother's clever and emotion-free capacity for argument, her daughter is healed and Easter is experienced. The miracle thus plays itself out in the dialogue! We could also say that in the moment of this rational argument the demonic forces lose their power.

Here is the essence of this scene: The gospel knows no limits, when it is that which is implied by its name: good news for *all* people and nations! In God's house there is enough room for everyone! Mark the evangelist thereby encourages his community and his readers to enter into dialogue with different cultures or, we can say, with the so-called pagans. By transcending boundaries, allowing himself to be corrected, and learning from this, Jesus is a model for the Christian community. We, too, should be an open learning community. What that means will be illustrated yet again in the ensuing scene (see Mark 7:31–37). Jesus heals a deaf-mute man and calls out to him, "Be opened!" That is what he himself has learned from the Syro-Phoenician woman. He thereby also addresses the reader: "Be opened! Don't be deaf when people like the foreign woman are God's messengers! Prick up your ears, move your tongue, and engage in conversation!"

FURTHER RENEWAL THROUGH A BOLD CHANGE OF PERSPECTIVE?

The many people fleeing their homes and in their plight seeking refuge in countries in Europe and America in some ways resemble the Syro-Phoenician woman who asks for her daughter to be healed and thus wishes for a healthy future. How many of these people flow into our homelands and beg for help! Here, too, it's a matter of their future.

Certainly it's a great challenge to take in so many people from other countries, and it's understandable that many meet these refugees with feelings of fear and negativity. They could, after all, take something away from us and lead to our being flooded with foreigners, so that there is literally no longer enough bread for our own children.

Precisely because of this it is helpful to change our perspective, like Jesus did, and to engage the foreign women in debate. Ultimately there is enough for everyone, and both sides could benefit from one another if there is willingness to coexist. The gospel encourages dialogue as well as assistance against all manipulative sensationalist propaganda that conjures up the end of Western civilization and its values.

Seen historically, Europe and North America have always changed through migration and people fleeing hardship and disaster. Thus we must ask ourselves honestly, What values are existential for our society, our country, and our continent? Finding a valid answer to this is very difficult when one observes how contentiously this theme is discussed.

But the example of the Syro-Phoenician woman strengthens us not to approach this in a confrontational manner, since it tends to conjure up fears and paint worst-case scenarios in black and white. Ultimately this is a dead end. Rather, our task is to start a constructive conversation about our values and together to seek solutions by rationally and calmly carrying on the dialogue. This all requires a patient approach to handling conflicts. In any case, border fences and walls don't stop globalization; rather, such measures fuel aggression, as we learn from the history of the great migrations in the fifth and sixth centuries, when the border walls of the Roman empire were overrun. Moreover, no one learns anything through isolation. In the long run, it's a much better solution to take the opportunity to shape globalization.

The example of Jesus learning from the Syro-Phoenician woman has consequences for the church. It is a motivation to interact openly with other religions and worldviews. Frequently enough, churches have radically destroyed foreign cultures, in many respects resembling the rampages of today's Islamic fundamentalists. Temples were maliciously destroyed and celebrations and religious rituals were forbidden under pain of punishment. The goal was to thoroughly eradicate paganism, which failed if we consider many forms of popular piety. In the Gospel, on the contrary, God reveals himself in the words of the foreign woman, who invites us to ask, Could God not also reveal himself through other religions? How much do we really know about the faith worlds of people who come to us from foreign lands?

The Syro-Phoenician woman who breaks into Jesus's faith world motivates us to respect what is sacred to other people, as required by freedom of religion and freedom of conscience. That doesn't mean that we must approve of everything, nor does it mean that we can't question anything. But this must be done carefully and judiciously.

To be sure, openness to objective dialogue requires a healthy self-awareness and knowledge of one's own claims, as Jesus proclaimed them for his own people, the people of Israel. For us Christians this means that Jesus of Nazareth is the Son of God or, as the Syro-Phoenician woman made known: For us he is Lord over life and death. In him God becomes visible. He is the salvation of humankind, as the Gospels demonstrate. It is our task to proclaim this boldly and confidently. In this context, Christianity was frequently a master of integration, accepting non-Christian rituals or ideas of popular piety and Christianizing them. The multiplicity of patron saints, for example, points to the ancient pantheon and is today interpreted as the plurality of God's forms of expression.

When we look back at the Gospels, it's very sad to see Christians closing off dialogue with other religions and worldviews because they claim salvation for themselves exclusively and attribute no validity to anything else. In the figurative sense such people are deaf and dumb. They are deaf because they no longer think that God can speak to them through other points of view. They are dumb because they close off the possibility of conversation. Inhuman forms of religious fundamentalism also have nothing in common with the gospel and the Jesus movement, which is open to all peoples. Rather, demonic powers that incite hate and violence among people with their extreme views are evident in them.

To be sure, Jesus frequently got involved in disputes and was convinced of his own teaching. He let himself be drawn into arguments with the scribes and religious leaders of his time. But the scene with the Syro-Phoenician woman shows that he did not slip into extreme positions but listened to what was being said. The woman received bread, that is, healing, so that her daughter was made whole again.

In the first multiplication of the loaves, Jesus challenged his disciples: "You give them something to eat" (Mark 6:37). In this we can find one of the enduring tasks of the church. Like the disciples, we must not shut ourselves off from the needs of our time, physical or spiritual. Rather, it is in the sharing that the miracle of healing occurs. In dialogue the demonic forces lose their power. If that isn't an encouragement to practice hospitality and to grapple reasonably with other worldviews! As a result of globalization, very many religious communities are represented in the large cities and urban areas. Could this not be an opportunity to learn something new in dialogue, but also in objective discussions to discover our own image anew?

In Mark's Gospel the articulate Syro-Phoenician woman gives the first impulse for the Jesus movement to be available to be open to other peoples and cultures rather than to limit itself to the people of Israel. Christianity has steadily made progress through such openness. Regarding this, consider the many women and men in our society today who are on a quest for meaning. Often they find no answers in established Christianity but instead are open to other religions or whatever else is available spiritually. I can think of many women among my acquaintances who, for example, practice yoga regularly. The physical and spiritual exercises help them to be at ease, and I'm amazed at the spiritual depths that they achieve through this. Much about such practices appears like Christian meditation and asceticism, while much is new and strange. But should we, on account of this, allow ourselves to judge the quality of these forms of inwardness? Couldn't God also reveal himself in such places where our traditional Christian home leaves off? The Syro-Phoenician woman's example is thought provoking, especially since her line of argument illustrates that women often have quite different approaches to reality than men have. If Jesus was taught something only by a woman, then today, too, God can choose unusual ways to touch us. It is important to be open especially to women's spirituality and forms of female mysticism. Why can't God, whom we confess as Creator of all that lives, also be revered as the divine Mother, as is the case in many nature religions? At least the Old Testament provides some tips. The Prophet Isaiah tells us that God would never forget his people, just as a mother does not forget her infant (see Isa 49:15), and that God comforts Israel like a mother does her child (see Isa 66:13). In Psalm 131 the Psalmist acknowledges that his soul comes to rest in God like a suckling child with its mother (Ps 131:2). Psalm 27 says, "If my father and mother forsake me, the LORD will take me up" (v. 10). St. Augustine (354–430), commenting on this verse, likens God to a mother "because he warms, he nourishes, he makes calm, he embraces." Some years ago these thoughts about the motherhood of God were incorporated into the liturgy. A Eucharistic Prayer on the theme of Jesus's care for the poor, sinners, and marginalized points out that his life and his message teach us that God cares for his children like a good father and a loving mother.

Can't the workings of God's spirit be described as female vitality, as Hildegard of Bingen (1098–1179) did by coining the word *viriditas*? In this invented word of uncertain origin are embedded such Latin words as *vir* (man), *virtus* (valor), *virga* (branch), *virgo* (virgin), *virginitas* (state of being untouched/unspoiled). It thereby designates a basic force that inhabits all of nature, thus humans, animals, plants, and minerals. According to

Hildegard, this basic force, which penetrates everything, is God's power and thus a life force that has healing effects. This can be applied as well to the workings of the Holy Spirit, who, as maternal, birthing force, continually confers health, healing, and new life. Next to the masculine-dominated trinitarian image of Father and Son, who are indeed always filled in from one's own experience of father and son, a female component would be added regarding the third Person of the Trinity. In turn, this corresponds to the Hebrew word for "spirit," *ruach*, which is feminine. At the same time, this concept represents breath and wind and thereby expresses yet again the life force that inhabits every living being. The Holy Spirit is thereby the bearer of life and helps us to better understand the feminine side of God.

In considering Jesus's openness to being corrected by a woman, it could be inspiring for men of the church to discover the concerns of feminine spirituality and so-called feminist theology as enrichment, rather than to dismiss them as "emancipatory" gimmicks. In the end, God will always remain the Incomprehensible, whose indescribability reflects the variety of existence. This means that God's being also has feminine characteristics.

Finally, all this touches on yet a further theme for the church. It is gratifying that in recent years, from the parish to the chancery, women have been able to participate in ecclesiastical life in an advisory role and with authority. In these areas much has already happened, thanks be to God, entirely within the church's tradition, which has repeatedly received new impulses through strong female figures. Thus, for example, Hildegard of Bingen, Teresa of Ávila (1515–82), and many other courageous women contributed to the life of the church, each in her own time. In fact, it was through the persistent influence of Catherine of Siena (1347–80) that the papacy returned from Avignon to Rome. Wouldn't it be appropriate and in accord with the gospel if women could be named cardinals, instead of limiting this honor only to those who have received the sacrament of orders, in other words, only to men? According to canon law this could be done with no problems, since over the centuries countless nonordained—thus lay—men were appointed cardinals and were among the closest colleagues and advisers to the popes. Only since 1917 has priestly ordination been a mandatory qualification for the cardinalate, thus reserving it for men. Think how enriching it would be if, for example, a dedicated grandmother, a nun experienced in the ways of the world, or a dynamic female manager with their life experiences were to have authority in the universal church. What would it mean if, in the future, not only men but experienced women as well could be eligible for the papacy? What qualifications would they bring to the Petrine office that men perhaps never consider?

In this context a single mother among my acquaintances comes to mind. When I hear the problems and challenges she must confront every day with her three adolescent children and the existential burdens that often occupy her—indeed, sometimes weigh on her—then so much in my own life is relativized. Every celibate, male-only club would profit from her down-to-earth life experiences in matters of family and youth work. She reminds me of the woman in the Gospel who cares for her daughter and about whose husband we know nothing. Was she, too, a single parent? At any rate, she encounters Jesus as a sole caregiver. How successfully could such women stand at the side of Peter's successor and serve the church in positions of responsibility through their keen perception of the reality of our lives!

In Mark's Gospel there is only one woman by whom Jesus lets himself be corrected and from whom he recognizes what is correct. Because of this he praises her response, which brings healing to her daughter and gives the girl a future and new life. In the church we must be open to the ways in which God is revealing himself today, even in the pope's innermost circle of advisers—because each person can become God's messenger, regardless of whether they are a woman or a man.

Chapter 5

A WOMAN TRUSTS WHOLEHEARTEDLY

I always love when cartoons, with few words, humorously put matters in a nutshell. Some time ago an acquaintance sent me a cartoon about ownership. There are two dogs: an older, fat dog that is chained up and lies wearily outside his doghouse, and a young, slim dog that is playing with a ball. The younger one enthusiastically calls to the older dog, "Come, play with me!" Meanwhile, the older dog has a thought balloon over his head that says, "That's what I used to think too, before I became a homeowner!"

The message is striking! Possession binds one. Ownership can not only make many things possible, but it can also limit our room to maneuver. I can identify with that cartoon in connection with our two monasteries. Since religious orders in Germany must finance themselves, conversations frequently revolve around the money and everything connected with it. That's true in our community as well. Topics such as the maintenance of two historically protected complexes in which something always requires repair, necessary investments in business enterprises, but also questions about personnel management, marketing, and so forth, dictate the agenda. In addition, equal attention must be given to financing and organizing not-for-profit projects such as our abbey library and our work for the homeless. This all requires time and energy. Sometimes I ask myself how it has come to this, since I entered monastic life specifically to leave these material concerns behind in order "to be free for God," in accord with our spirituality. Now, however, I occasionally resemble that dog on a chain.

The cartoon makes this point: We can be ambivalent about ownership and property. On the one hand, they can ensure and safeguard outer freedom, so that, for example, a monastery does not depend on contributors. At the same time, generous donations and gifts can all too easily result in uncomfortable obligations. To counteract this, St. Benedict wants his monks to earn their living by the work of their hands (see RB 48.8). Economic self-sufficiency (autarchy) should ensure the monastery's independence (autonomy).

On the other hand, ownership and property can make one unfree and lead to obsession, so that people define themselves only by what they own and try to acquire more and more wealth. Thus St. Benedict warns against the vice of greed and recommends that the products of the monastery be sold at a more favorable price than those of the competition, "so that in all things God may be glorified" (RB 57.9).

This is certainly not always possible. One of my predecessors, Abbot Hugo Lang (1892–1967), was once asked why, then, is our beer somewhat more expensive than that of the other breweries since this does not follow the recommendation of the *Rule*. Abbot Hugo is said to have quick-wittedly replied, "To guarantee the high quality of the product, which costs more to manufacture. Our beer isn't cheaper, but it is therefore better!" Ultimately even monastic enterprises compete with other businesses and need to face this to ensure the community's financial grounding. This is understandable, yet the crucial question remains: How does this accord with one's lifestyle? Is it credible?

The vow of fidelity to the monastic way of life (*conversatio morum*) that we Benedictines take involves both the community property and personal poverty. Of course, Benedict wants the monk to have everything he needs for his life (see RB 34), but sometimes it's not easy to decide what this is. Do I really need to have my own car, my own desk, my own computer? How do I handle the possibility of others' claims on them? Can I share them with others? Would it be difficult for me to let go of these things?

In the end it's a matter of connection and trust in God, as the dedication of one's life during profession makes clear. When I entered monastic life, an older brother asked me if I planned to stay. I answered evasively and very uncertainly, "Time will tell... but first comes the novitiate!" The brother replied, "There's no such thing as a little bit pregnant!" This thought has motivated me ever since. Am I prepared to place my trust in God again and again and not to rely on other means of security? Using a widow as an example, Jesus conceptualizes for his disciples what that means.

THE GENEROUS WIDOW

> He sat down opposite the treasury, and watched the crowd putting money into the treasury. Many rich people put in large sums. A poor widow came and put in two small copper coins, which are worth a penny. Then he called his disciples and said to them, "Truly I tell you, this poor widow has put in more than all those who are contributing to the treasury. For all of them have contributed out of their abundance; but she out of her poverty has put in everything she had, all she had to live on." (Mark 12:41–44)

This brief scene takes place in the temple in Jerusalem. Jesus had left his home in Galilee and gone up to the City of David with his disciples. After his celebrated entry into Jerusalem, he angrily drove the merchants and vendors out of the temple. He reproached them for making the house of God a den of thieves (see Mark 11:15–18). Business should not be carried on in the place where one meets God!

Yet, it should not be forgotten that the temple had an important economic role. Like any place of pilgrimage, it, too, was a lucrative source of income. The buildings, after all, had to be maintained and the priests and employees paid. The expulsion of the merchants and vendors was thus an authentic provocation through which Jesus challenged the economic operations of the temple. Not money but God should be put back in the center. In this place service should be rendered to God alone.

The consequence was a renewal of vehement conflicts with the religious authorities. There followed debates with the Pharisees, the Sadducees, and the scribes on such topics as taxes, resurrection, and authority. The atmosphere became increasingly heated, and for Jesus the situation escalated dangerously.

Just before the brief scene with the widow, Jesus had leveled some sharp criticisms at the demeanor of the scribes. He warned emphatically about their corrupt greed and their unmatched hypocrisy: "Beware of the scribes, who like to walk around in long robes, and to be greeted with respect in the marketplaces, and to have the best seats in the synagogues and places of honor at banquets! They devour widows' houses and for the sake of appearance say long prayers. They will receive the greater condemnation" (Mark 12:38–40). The word *devour* is a literal translation from the Greek. Jesus thereby portrays the scribes in a sharp contrast to the poor widow, whose unreserved dedication he highlights as exemplary in direct connection with his criticism. In today's money, her gift of two small coins would equal about a penny. If that represents what she had to subsist on, she certainly belonged to the poor underclass.

The contrasts are striking: Here the distinguished upper-class scribes, there a little-noticed widow at the margins of society; here the religious professionals who teach and pray with many words, there a simple pious woman who remains voiceless among those who go unnoticed; here the rich men who greedily seek their own advantage, there a poor woman who with complete trust in God contributes all that she has to live on. Ultimately this is a contrast between appearing and being, so that the poor widow, through Jesus's praise, takes the place of the scribes. While the latter love only themselves, she gives everything for God. Through her action this woman teaches what the kingdom of God is all about.

At the same time, the generous gifts of the wealthy are initially regarded with approval. But in the end, it's not the amount of the gift that's decisive. While those who are well-off only contribute from their surplus, without "giving until it hurts," the widow, with the coins she has saved, sacrifices "her entire life," as the Greek text says. She doesn't even keep one of the two coins for herself but puts all that she has into the temple treasury. Ultimately, she unreservedly entrusts her life to God!

The essence of this brief instruction to the disciples is this: It is not the size of the gift that is decisive, but the sincerity of the giver's disposition. In the end this poor widow has, without realizing it, understood more about the kingdom of God than the educated teachers of Israel. God's kingdom can't be bought, but one can give one's life for it, as Jesus offered himself on the cross (see Mark 10:45).

By giving all that she had for the temple in deep trust in God and thereby freeing her heart from all material comforts, she herself becomes the temple, that is, the dwelling place of God.

Directly in connection with this scene Jesus will predict the destruction of the massive temple, whose treasures the disciples had been admiring. No stone will remain upon another (see Mark 13:1–2). None of its splendor will endure. Everything will be destroyed. Thus, the disciples should, rather, hold to Jesus and his words. Again and again the message is unreserved trust in God, which the widow has modeled.

In this connection, this woman likewise stands in contrast to a rich man that Jesus had met earlier on his way to Jerusalem (see Mark 10:17–27). He had asked Jesus, "Good Teacher, what must I do to inherit eternal life?" (Mark 10:17). According to his own testimony, he had followed from his youth all the commands that Jesus enumerated for him in reply. He was already living a model life. At that, as the Gospel poignantly tells us, "Jesus, looking at him, loved him and said, 'You lack one thing; go, sell what you own, and give the money to the poor, and you will have treasure in heaven; then come, follow me'" (Mark 10:21). To give up everything for love—the wealthy man could not do this, and so, the Gospel says, he went away sad. Jesus's comment on this has become a proverb: "Then Jesus looked around and said to his disciples, 'How hard it will be for those who have wealth to enter the kingdom of God!...It is easier for a camel to go through the eye of a needle than for someone who is rich to enter the kingdom of God'" (Mark 10:23, 25). The widow, in contrast, had let go of her possessions and placed her life in the temple treasury. That is the freedom that should distinguish the disciple.

Finally, this underscores the scene following the encounter with the rich man. Referring to this inability to let go of everything, Peter declares to Jesus, "Look, we have left everything and followed you" (Mark 10:28). Jesus replies, "Truly I tell you, there is no one who has left house or brothers or sisters or mother or father or children or fields, for my sake and for the sake of the good news, who will not receive a hundredfold now in this age—houses, brothers and sisters, mothers and children, and fields, with persecutions—and in the age to come eternal life. But many who are first will be last, and the last will be first" (Mark 10:29–31).

Through her devotion, this anonymous widow has unknowingly joined the group of disciples, as described in the Book of Deuteronomy: "Hear, O Israel: The Lord is our God, the Lord alone. You shall love the LORD your God with all your heart, and with all your soul, and with all your might" (Deut 6:4–5). Shortly before the encounter with the widow, Jesus had expanded this command to love God to include love of neighbor. Whoever is prepared to give their life for God and their neighbor is, consciously or unconsciously, not far from the kingdom of God (see Mark 12:28–34). For God is not impressed by the size of a gift; rather, he is concerned with all of what he sees in a person's heart. The widow's example is a critical question to the disciples of every era: Where is a temple-cleansing of the heart needed? God's kingdom cannot be purchased, but one can abandon oneself to it. Our becoming the temple, the dwelling place of God, depends upon this greatness of heart!

INCREASED CREDIBILITY THROUGH REFORM OF CHURCH COLLECTIONS?

The Catholic Church may well seem to many observers more like a rich widow than a poor one. Thus it's not surprising that discussions arise about the church and its wealth. Naturally, much good is accomplished with the church's resources, when one considers its extensive engagement in care for souls, its social and educational projects, or the costly maintenance of cultural monuments. Churches—not only the Catholic Church—are among the largest employers and run their own kindergartens and daycare centers, schools, educational institutions, clinics, all kinds of social institutions, and much more.

Much of this, however, is seen as a burden in the sense of the cartoon described above, so that even those with responsibility in the church are demanding a "detachment from the world." What should we let go of? What should we unreservedly, and with the greatest trust in God, sacrifice, like the widow in the story did, to become freer? Where might even a cleansing of the temple be necessary in order for us to fulfill our mission more credibly once again?

Again and again I meet people who have left the church but declare that they believe in Jesus and his message. The reasons for this are varied. Frequently the need to save money (by not feeling compelled to tithe) is given as a reason.*

Often, however, someone will express pent-up anger about the "institutional church" or disappointment with pastors or other church personnel, including deep harm, as, for example, through sexual abuse or force. Others share that they have entirely separated themselves from the life of the church and live their faith in Jesus privately.

The consequences of leaving the church—independently of the reasons—are clear. Among them are exclusion from the sacraments and prohibition from being a godparent or sponsor at a baptism or confirmation. Also, someone who has left the church will hardly be able to find employment with a church or a church agency. Unfortunately, it's natural that such punishments leveled at people to whom Jesus and his gospel still mean something are less likely to result in a return than to cause new resentment and additional hurt. Many such people will not see the church as a locus of lived faith and mercy but as a wealthy institution that demands financial contributions of its members. As they see it, the church is more like the Pharisees, who seek their own advantage, than the poor widow whom Jesus praised because of her generosity.

Because of this situation, which leads further and further away from the core of the gospel, the inevitable question arises: How would it be if the church imitated the widow in Mark's Gospel and, without reservation, left open the question of contributions? How would it be if the individual Christian could decide freely where their contribution would be applied, whether

* Editor's note: In the author's country, Germany, churches are financed by a tax imposed on registered members by the government.

to the school, the homeless, or the maintenance of a cathedral, for example?

For one thing, this would lead to unbundling (i.e., a separation between management and accounting), since the church membership, which indissolubly exists through the sacrament of baptism, would no longer be dependent on a mandatory contribution such as tithing. No longer would someone have to leave the church because of money. For another, the church would become poorer and would lose social influence as well as political power. But would it not thereby conform to the example of the poor widow and be freer?

Let's take this idea a bit further. Abandoning mandatory contributions such as tithing would result in many internal changes in the church. Diocesan leadership and communities would have to reflect on which establishments they could continue to operate, and which would have to be left to other institutions or, indeed, given up. Many things would have to be absorbed by the state and by society and reorganized. For the church, this would mean a painful process of letting go. But it could also be an act of liberation if we think of the consequences of secularization at the beginning of the nineteenth century. At that time, churches in Europe had their property confiscated by the state, and monasteries and religious orders were dissolved. This painful and compulsory expropriation brought about a surprising upswing. New orders, associations, initiatives, and movements arose, so that church life was reawakened to new life in the middle of the nineteenth century.

This upswing actually corresponded with the heraldic motto of our mother monastery, Monte Cassino: *Sucissa virescit!*—"Cut down, it grows back stronger!" The verse refers to the shifting fate of this monastery, which over the course of its long history was destroyed several times but thereafter arose again. Like a dead tree stump, sprung from the tender shoot, monastic life at Monte

Cassino gained strength again and again. Couldn't this also work today for a poorer church?

Soberly considered, abandoning mandatory contributions could result in increased truthfulness. Perhaps one example will serve as clarification: Frequently not much Christian attitude can be sensed in a church-sponsored clinic, because the shortage of vocations has led to a lack of religious sisters. It's usually the case that those who manage these hospitals suffer from the same economic pressures as other religious houses. Beds can no longer be occupied for as long. Private patients are given priority treatment because they bring money to the clinic. Nursing measures are timed to save energy. Cleaning duties are outsourced to independent firms to save on expenses. And the list goes on. The same is true for all other church institutions that were once founded in the charismatic spirit of devotion and love of neighbor but are now managed as social concerns. Wouldn't it be more honest to let go of these ventures and start anew on a small scale?

It would be interesting to see if new initiatives would then emerge in our own time. Perhaps a circle of people would form that, motivated by Christian values, would support a clinic by helping to distribute meals or provide simple care. Possibly a group of like-minded parents would get together to start their own kindergarten with a Christian orientation. In a sense, by being involved in this way they would be imitating the poor widow and dropping a part of their life into the poor box.

Their example might motivate others to get involved by offering according to their own charisms. This spiritual reconsideration of the question "Where am I called to offer my abilities in the community?" would be something quite different from the comfortable attitude, "I put my envelope in the collection every week, so in return I get the church services of baptism, marriage, and burial."

In this context it's equally important to question the credibility of church labor rules. Should we not place these, too, in the poor box? Clearly it would be desirable if church institutions were staffed by workers who live active Christian lives. Equally, it is understandable that employees should have a fundamental loyalty to their employer's values. But then comes the question of whether Christian faith must be a condition of employment in all church-sponsored institutions, especially since, viewed realistically, employees with this mindset aren't easy to find. To be sure, their baptismal certificate indicates that they are members of the church, but it's also known that, in the end, true Christian conviction can't be legally required. It's either given or not! Here, too, the question of being versus appearing arises.

On the one hand, Jesus accused the Pharisees of hypocrisy, and on the other, he praised the widow's dedication. Are we not fostering the former situation if, say, a young woman who wants to be a religion teacher feels compelled to become involved in the parish in order to get a good referral from her pastor, but then, after she begins her employment, quietly pulls back? Does this also not apply to many moral standards that shape the church's labor rules, so that employees who wish to live their faith in their work as well must, for example, keep quiet about the fact that they are cohabiting or would like to marry their homosexual partner?

The widow's example shows that the kingdom of God cannot be bought according to a profit-and-loss statement. Nor can this be disputed before the labor tribunals. Really, it comes down to commitment because true love neither calculates nor counts.

Many fathers of the church have compared the church to a widow. I like this image because widowed people frequently carry on the legacy of their deceased spouse. Freya von Moltke (1911–2010), for example, whose husband was executed on January 23, 1941, as a resistance fighter, stood up for her husband's legacy throughout her long life. Many contemporaries who spoke with her got the impression that an invisible person was sitting with them at the table. This, really, is precisely the church's task: In our speech and actions the invisible presence of the Risen One must be felt at our table. That is, of course, a high aspiration.

The widow gave away what she had to live on. And we: For what do we live? For what do we use our life? What is our sacred place, our temple? Hopefully, not the church's labor laws and the collection plate.

Chapter 6

A WOMAN SQUANDERS SOMETHING BEAUTIFUL

An internet advertisement for a popular hand cream proclaims, "Gentle contact creates wellness, harmony, and confidence. It brings more light to the day. Tender touches build up strong connections and are passed on from one generation to the next." These sentences may sound somewhat effusive, and yet they express something true: Our skin is a sensitive organ. Through our skin we encounter others and form relationships. We greet people by shaking hands with them or, if we have a closer connection to a person, we embrace. Lovers kiss and yearn for physical union. Children need to take their parent's hand when they're afraid, or receive a gentle caress when they are sad.

Touch shapes our lives. Touches occur externally, of course, but also within. When, for example, we declare, "That touched me deeply!" then perhaps it's a magnificent sunset or beautiful music that, in the truest sense of the word, has gotten "under our skin." Many forms of touch can heal and comfort. They are "balm for the soul," as we gratefully declare.

When we are deeply touched, we are often experiencing something very good or very beautiful. This is how we come close to God's mystery, in which perfect goodness and beauty are united. In such moments, in which time stands still, so to speak, we enjoy something of eternal happiness.

Again and again this means that even with our help God can touch people in their innermost being when we do something good and beautiful. In this way the beautiful is, in a sense, an enhancement of the good, as the pastor-poet Kurt Marti (1921–2017) says: "One should do good, but one can also do something beautiful. Good deeds give meaning to life. Beautiful deeds make life shine. Beautiful deeds are the cherry on the cake of good deeds!" His thoughts often recall a poem by Hilde Domin (1909–2006) titled *Die Heiligen* (The Saints), in which the poet, regarding the beauty of the fine arts, states, "For we eat bread, but we live on grandeur."

The beauty of many works of art can touch us deeply in our innermost being. Nothing else is of concern when some churches are richly furnished with art. Looking at many a valuable artistic treasure, the critical question will certainly be asked, What good could be done with all this?

A key word in our *Rule* helps me here. In the chapter on obedience, Benedict cites the Apostle Paul: "God loves a cheerful giver" (see 2 Cor 9:7; RB 5.16). In saying this, Paul wanted to motivate the Corinthians to contribute generously to the church in Jerusalem. For Benedict, the monk must not go through life morose and mumbling but entrust his life to God with a joyful heart. This can readily be applied to many a good deed and, equally, to many a beautiful work: "For we eat bread, but we live on grandeur."

To refer again to the slogan cited at the beginning, the goodness and the beauty of a joyful heart can lead to the most beautiful kind of touch. Jesus experienced this shortly before his death in the encounter with a woman whose lavish deed was like balm for his soul.

THE MAGNANIMOUS ADMIRER

> While he was at Bethany in the house of Simon the leper, as he sat at the table, a woman came with an alabaster jar of very costly ointment of nard, and she broke open the jar and poured the ointment on his head. But some were there who said to one another in anger, "Why was the ointment wasted in this way? For this ointment could have been sold for more than three hundred denarii, and the money given to the poor." And they scolded her. But Jesus said, "Let her alone; why do you trouble her? She has performed a good service for me. For you always have the poor with you, and you can show kindness to them whenever you wish; but you will not always have me. She has done what she could; she has anointed my body beforehand for its burial. Truly I tell you, wherever the good news is proclaimed in the whole world, what she has done will be told in remembrance of her." (Mark 14:3–9)

Unfortunately, this story is never read in a usual Sunday Mass, and consequently the self-confident woman whose generous act is praised as an integral part of the Gospel probably turns up rarely as a topic for preaching. Only once every three years, if the long version of St. Mark's account of the passion is proclaimed, do we hear about her, and then this touching scene at the start of the passion assumes a top position. While the shadows of death close in on the life of Jesus, a woman shines through her good work. The event even corresponds with the Easter narrative at the end of the Gospel. At the beginning and at the end of the passion story we meet women who wish to honor Jesus by anointing him.

At the same time, a grim frame surrounds the present scene. Earlier the high priests and scribes had decided that they wanted to kill Jesus. They would use cunning to quietly bring him into their power. After the anointing, Judas Iscariot declares himself ready to deliver Jesus to them at an opportune time. The contrast could not be greater: on the one side aggressive hatred and contempt, on the other side a demonstration of deepest reverence and esteem.

Jesus is in Bethany, a guest in the house of Simon the leper. This village before the gates of the city probably served as his residence and place of retreat during his visits to Jerusalem (see Mark 11:11, 19). The privacy of a house serves again and again as a place of instruction for the disciples and, equally, for us as well. Jesus is invited for a meal and, completely unexpectedly, a woman intrudes into this male-only club that constituted Jewish table fellowship in Jesus's time. Undaunted, she breaches the rules of propriety and does what she considers right. Today we would call her an emancipated woman. Like the Syro-Phoenician woman before her, she, too, approaches Jesus freely and unconventionally. And like the woman who suffered from a hemorrhage, she self-confidently takes the initiative and anoints him by breaking an alabaster vessel above his head. She uses the valuable perfume not to make herself shine but to honor the guest from Nazareth.

This is the only anointing that Jesus receives in Mark's Gospel. In fact, the woman's action makes him the Anointed One, in Hebrew, *Messiah*; in Greek, *Christ*. Mark had given him this title at the very beginning of his Gospel (see Mark 1:1). Analogously, Peter later declares, "You are the Messiah" (Mark 8:29).

The yearning of the people of Israel for a savior who would appear at the end-time is tied in with this anointing. The Jewish kingdom came to an end with the Babylonian captivity around 586 BCE. Since that time, the prophets increasingly developed the notion of an apocalyptic redeemer whose coming would transform everything. This messiah would be a person chosen by God, thus the Lord's anointed one who, by establishing the kingdom of God, would bring about a radical and final turn of events.

He is repeatedly sung about as such in the psalms (see Pss 2:2; 20:7; 45:8; 89:10, 21, 39, 52; 132:10, 17). This would all resonate with the knowledgeable reader when Mark's Gospel describes this woman's surprising action.

The anointing of Jesus's head also recalls the prophet Samuel's anointings of Saul and David as king (see 1 Sam 10:1; 16). Does this woman also perform on Jesus a prophetic service normally reserved for men? Does she see in Jesus the expected messiah? Or is it simply an act of esteem, or an expression of her extravagant devotion and love, as many exegetes believe? The answer remains in the dark and the meaning for us readers is open to interpretation. In any case, the woman anoints his head and not his feet, as other Gospels describe it (see Luke 7:38; John 11:1–10). The original Greek text, too, lacks any mention of hair, as it is often translated. The anointing of the head is anything other than an act of submission!

Of course, anointings were a part of everyday life in the ancient East. They could serve hygienic and cosmetic purposes. Guests used them to refresh and pamper themselves. For sick people they served for cleansing and healing, as even Jesus's disciples did (see Mark 6:13). Corpses were anointed to honor the deceased.

In the end, this all comes together when this emancipated woman pours the expensive nard over Jesus. The stated value of three hundred denarii is considerable, a sum equal to the annual income of a worker at that time.

Her behavior must have been provocative, and thus it is understandable that her spontaneous action was criticized by the men who were present and dismissed as a waste of money. Think of the things that the money could have been used for! Was that necessary? These objections remind us a bit of the encounter with the rich man of whom the previous chapter spoke. Jesus had invited him, "Go, sell what you own, and give the money to the poor, and you will have treasure in heaven; then come, follow me" (Mark 10:21). But the man wasn't prepared to give everything up, and he went away sad. The generous woman with her costly ointment is, like the widow in the temple, the antithesis of the rich man.

Had the men with their criticism taken to heart the example of the poor widow whose generous deed Jesus praised as exemplary? We don't know. In any case, they reproach the woman severely. She, however, remains silent throughout the scene and doesn't defend herself. Is it an expression of her authority, that she is convinced of the correctness of her action and has no need of justification? Or has the sharp criticism intimidated her into silence? The evangelist leaves this, too, an open question. He regards other things as more important.

Jesus is visibly touched by the woman's extravagant act. We could almost say that the anointing has "gotten under his skin" and is balm for his soul amid what is hanging over him. Thus he vehemently protects the woman and defends what she has done. He speaks about the good deed she has performed for him. It recalls the Creation story in Genesis (see 1:1—2:4): at the end of each day God looks at his new work and sees that it was good. In the Greek translation of the Hebrew original, the word *kalos* is used here, which also means "beautiful." It could also be translated "it was beautiful." This thought can be pursued more deeply.

The German word *schön* (beautiful) comes from *schauen* (to look), which is related to the English word *show*. Therefore, when I look at someone and show them respect, then in my eyes they are beautiful. We could apply this as well to God's work of creation. God's respect for his work makes it beautiful: "And God looked at everything and it was very beautiful!"

The respect that the woman showed Jesus by anointing him did him good. It made him beautiful. Thus he praised the good work, the woman's beautiful action. We could even say that she imitated God the Creator and lavishly bestowed life. This thought, too, can be developed further: What this woman does at the beginning of Jesus's passion will, through God, have an effect on Easter. Even in death he looks at his Son. He shows him respect and awakens new life in him. Through this beautiful act, Jesus is confirmed as Messiah. He is the beloved Son. The Father is well pleased with him, as was already said at Jesus's baptism, as told at the beginning of the Gospel (see Mark 1:11).

God's respect is stronger than death! Thus, the anointing by the woman can be interpreted as a paschal deed. She self-confidently sets her action in opposition to the passion. Indeed, Jesus has not fulfilled his people's expectations of the messiah. He is no political messiah. Rather, he follows the notion of the suffering messiah, who, by his death on the cross, acts in solidarity with humankind. This is the outer limit of self-sacrifice (see Mark 10:45). Is this what the woman wanted to point out with her lavish gift? At any rate, this seems to be so when Jesus states that the woman "has done what she could; she has anointed my body beforehand for its burial" (Mark 14:8). She has recognized the Kairos moment and seized the opportunity by anointing him as the Messiah. Her beautiful deed crowns him amid his suffering. In this connection it is interesting that strong calming and anxiety-reducing properties are attributed to nard. Did the woman perhaps intend her anointing to prepare Jesus for the passion and death that awaited him? This question, too, is left open by the evangelist.

Conversely, Jesus, with a slightly ironic undertone, admonishes the men who are present, "For you always have the poor with you" (Mark 14:7). That is, the critics always have opportunities to do good for those who are in need. Bethany—the place where the poor live—is everywhere! But while Jesus was still alive, they would have had the chance to do good and beautiful things for him in the face of death: "For we eat bread, but we live on grandeur." We can't help asking, Is their criticism really about care for the poor or about maligning the woman's extravagant reverence and provocative appreciation? Could the men be jealous of Jesus? Here, too, there are no answers.

The men's reaction is reminiscent of another scene in Mark's Gospel in which the Pharisees critically inquire why Jesus's disciples don't fast. Jesus counters with another question: "The wedding guests cannot fast while the bridegroom is with them, can they? As long as they have the bridegroom with them, they cannot fast. The days will come when the bridegroom is taken away from them, and then they will fast on that day" (Mark 2:19–20). In this connection, Jesus had healed a man on the Sabbath and further intensified the conflict with the Pharisees by asking them whether it was permitted to do good or to do evil on the Sabbath, to save a life or to kill. Full of anger and sorrow over their hardened hearts, Jesus looks around at them all and heals the man. In turn, this results in the Pharisees' first decision to bring Jesus down (see Mark 3:6).

With this background, the way Jesus interprets the woman's "good deed" is revealing: "She has anointed my body beforehand for its burial" (Mark 14:8). For Jesus the magnanimous act is a sign of solidarity. It is an act of love performed for a doomed man on whom the woman nevertheless bestows her total veneration. It may be extravagant to anoint a dead person; after all, the deceased doesn't profit from it. And yet it expresses high esteem.

As with the widow in the temple, Jesus emphasizes with an "Amen" the noteworthy meaning of this action: "Wherever the good news is proclaimed in the whole world, what she has done will be told in remembrance of her" (Mark 14:9). Thus, the message of the anointing is aimed at the public, those who will hear the gospel preached, and only here does Mark mention remembrance. The woman's act of anointing uniquely combines memory and proclamation. Through her good and beautiful action, this woman shines amid death and the tomb. Thereby, she has ultimately, whether consciously or otherwise, continued the writing of the gospel in her life. In this, she is an example for each reader and each Christian community. What happened in the insignificant village of Bethany has abiding and worldwide significance, for the gospel consists not so much of abstract truths of faith as of touching encounters that get under one's skin. Jesus experiences this in Bethany. But through this, amid the shadows of death, the Easter message of life to the fullest shines radiantly. Everything that we, like this woman, magnanimously do that is good and beautiful without it being asked or expected of us gives our life sparkle. In the end, God's presence beams through such acts because God loves a cheerful giver! Good and beautiful acts don't often pay off, but they are good news. So we should always ask ourselves, Where is Bethany—the place where the poor live—today? Where are we, as a church, asked to give extravagant brilliance to life through good works and beautiful deeds? Who benefits from our balm for the soul? Who would be made beautiful by our respect?

CAN WE IMPROVE PASTORAL CARE BY EXPANDING THE CONCEPT OF "SACRAMENT"?

If we continue considering the anointing at Bethany in the context of Christian ecumenism, we can sketch it out as follows: Because of the divisions brought about by the Reformation, the one Body of Christ is wounded and broken. It resembles the body of Jesus in the passion. In recent centuries, thank God, much has been accomplished—for example, the different denominations recognize one another's baptisms and Christians of different confessions can worship together. Many wounds have been healed; others remain open. Thus, for example, Protestants are not allowed to receive the Eucharist at Catholic services.

The Gospel shows that Jesus had no fears about being touched. His anointing at Bethany reminds us of the anointing with chrism after baptism, when the newly baptized is told, "[God] now anoints you with the chrism of salvation. As Christ was anointed Priest, Prophet, and King, so may you live always as a member of his body, sharing everlasting life" (Rite of Baptism). Through the sacrament, each baptized person belongs to Christ forever. That is a big truth whose significance can scarcely be comprehended. If we believe that the risen Christ is present with his flesh and blood in bread and wine, can we deny access to communion to a Christian who, through their baptism, belongs forever to Christ? True, there are evangelical Christians for whom the Lord's Supper is merely symbolic and who don't believe in the Real Presence. However, at the Lord's Supper they receive the bread and wine with respect and reverence. Would Jesus, who we believe is present in the sacrament of the Eucharist, have feared being touched by people who belong to him on account of their baptism? Would he not wish to be their guest as well, even unrecognized? Ultimately, would that not be healing balm for the wounded Body of the Lord?

Regarding the anointing with chrism after baptism, a path opens to a quite different topic: A while ago I was invited to the home of a homosexual couple. Both men attend Sunday Mass regularly and come from good Catholic families. During our conversation they expressed the wish to be married in church with me presiding. They were convinced of their love for each other and that their love witnessed to God's love. They were firmly determined to accompany each other faithfully and bindingly through life, and they wished to recognize God as the third member in their partnership. They didn't want to settle for a blessing. They wanted to form a full-fledged mutual bond for life and to promise each other lifelong faithfulness before God.

I began by replying that a church marriage also included being prepared to have children together. This argument didn't hold water, however, because one of the men then asked me with a smile what I would do with a couple in which both bride and groom were already more than seventy years old and certainly were no longer able to have children. We sat together for a long time, deep in conversation, and in the course of it, it became increasingly clear to me how serious was the wish they expressed. I was overcome by sorrow because as a pastor I couldn't help them further. On the way home I thought of the rich man who wasn't prepared to give his all but sadly went away.

Since that meeting I think often of these two men and my inability to help them, which at the same time reflects the helplessness of our church. Are we not richly gifted with the gospel and yet often not able to lavish brilliance through it on life with its concrete challenges?

According to church teaching, marriage is limited to a union between a man and a woman, as established in the Bible. But none of this entitles us to condemn the love between two men or two women. Love and devotion are present in these relationships! And so the question arises: How could we serve homosexual couples, who have often suffered under the church's teaching and left the church, through a beautiful act? How could we pour over them the expensive nard, not patronizingly but generously?

Ever since the encounter described above, I've been giving room to my thoughts, using as a model the self-assured woman in Bethany. She followed her conscience and did what she considered right. Perhaps what's needed for homosexual couples is their own liturgical ritual based on Psalm 133:

> How very good and pleasant it is
>   when kindred live together in unity!
> It is like the precious oil on the head,
>   running down upon the beard,
> on the beard of Aaron,
>   running down over the collar of his robes.
> It is like the dew of Hermon,
>   which falls on the mountains of Zion.
> For there the Lord ordained his blessing,
>   life forevermore.

Couldn't the church, in accordance with this psalm and the anointing of Jesus in Bethany, develop a ritual of brotherhood or sisterhood in which homosexual couples are anointed with oil, or anoint each other, and thus can enter a binding partnership? It would be an exciting project if affected couples, pastors, and liturgists were involved in the conversation.

Anointing rituals could be important for other groups as well. Here, too, it would be worth it to think about creative developments of the sacraments. Again and again in my pastoral work, I meet people whose lives are characterized by great sorrow. Some have suffered the loss of someone dear to them or a broken relationship; others have lost their employment, while still others have failed in life and are having trouble dealing with a difficult fate. Often, resignation and weariness of life increase. Sometimes a visible sign of God's loving care would be helpful in these tricky situations. Couldn't an "anointing of the sorrowful," corresponding to the anointing of the sick as balm for the soul, be a good work that comforts and raises up? Psalm 147 says, "He heals the broken-hearted, / and binds up their wounds" (Ps 147:3). Wasn't the anointing in Bethany also a sign of comfort for Jesus in a difficult situation?

How beautiful it would be, in the spirit of the sacrament of confirmation, if we had a ritual of encouragement for people in crisis. The anointing could be accompanied by the words: "Have no fear! Even if a dark valley lies before you! Even if you don't know how you should decide, but instead have the impression, 'It's all the same what I do, it can only be wrong…,' God does not leave you alone!" Similarly, there are people enmeshed in difficult conflicts who are occasionally exposed to evil tendencies and thoughts. Here, too, it would be helpful if we could counter this with a visible sign. A text from Psalm 20 can support this sign when addressed to the person being anointed:

> Now I know that the Lord will help his anointed;
> he will answer him from his holy heaven
> with mighty victories by his right hand.
> Some take pride in chariots, and some in horses,
> but our pride is in the name of the Lord our God.
> They will collapse and fall,
> but we shall rise and stand upright. (Ps 20:6–8)

Did Jesus not experience this himself through his death and resurrection?

What further beautiful actions, what rituals of anointing as balm for the soul could be offered, loosely based on the rite of priestly ordination, for those who have responsibility in the life of the church but also in society in general? Once again, a point of connection would be baptism, in which the anointed person is reminded of the office of priest, prophet, and king. Simply a close study of Psalm 23, "The Lord is my shepherd," yields many suggestions about what it means not to become arrogant in one's role, but always to seek reassurance from the One from whom all power derives:

> The Lord is my shepherd, I shall not want.
> He makes me lie down in green pastures;
> he leads me beside still waters;
> he restores my soul.
> He leads me in right paths
> for his name's sake.
>
> Even though I walk through the darkest valley,
> I fear no evil;
> for you are with me;
> your rod and your staff—
> they comfort me.

> You prepare a table before me
>   in the presence of my enemies;
> you anoint my head with oil;
>   my cup overflows.
> Surely goodness and mercy shall follow me
>   all the days of my life,
> and I shall dwell in the house of the LORD
>   my whole life long.

Even just the images in this psalm offer some starting points from which touching rituals could be creatively developed.

It would be exciting to search for clues in the Bible, based on the extravagant act of the woman at Bethany. The Council of Lyons (1274) fixed the number of sacraments at seven. But in the preceding centuries the number wasn't so clearly defined. For example, both Ambrose of Milan (339–97) and Bernard of Clairvaux (1090–1153) considered foot washing to be a sacrament of forgiveness. Nor had it been conclusively agreed whether the anointing of kings and queens with chrism had a sacramental character. The same was true of the consecration of abbots as a form of episcopal ordination, so that many abbots were ordained as priests for their monasteries as a matter of course. Nor should we forget ordination to minor orders, such as the subdiaconate, which were abolished with the liturgical reforms of Vatican II. Based on these historical facts, would it not be possible for the church, aided by the Holy Spirit and in accord with the signs of the times, to discover new sacraments that have a basis in the Bible?

This could be applied similarly to further church offices. Certainly it requires courage to increase the rich treasure of the church and generously allow others to participate. Perhaps it would help to keep in mind the anxiety-reducing properties of nard.

In any case, Jesus praised the extravagant gift of the woman at Bethany as a beautiful act and promised that her memory would live on in the gospel. The woman's example invites us, at least in our thoughts, to lavish the expensive oil of anointing on the body of Christ. If further beautiful acts arise from this, then the poet's words would be fulfilled: "For we eat bread, but we live on grandeur." All this could bring much joy and have life-giving effects for the church in accordance with the conviction that God loves a cheerful giver.

CONCLUSION

Let Us Set Out with the Gospel for Our Guide!

While this book was in development, I told a friend about the critical questions provoked by the six women. He spontaneously replied, "Just make sure that you don't become evangelical!"* His humorous reaction started me thinking. Actually, it would be nice if we—the Catholic Church—could become a little more "evangelical" through the provocative women in Mark's Gospel. The Latin word for "evangelical"—*evangelicus*—originally meant "corresponding to the message of the gospel." It's in this sense that we speak of the "evangelical counsels" in connection with the vows taken by religious. Understood in that way, to become evangelical would mean to serve the church and to comply with St. Benedict's instruction when he writes in the prologue to our *Rule*, "Let us set out on this way [of life shown by the Lord], with the Gospel for our guide" (RB Prol. 21). This, in turn, would

* The term *evangelisch* in German usually means "Protestant" in the first instance—not "evangelical" in the sense in which Americans normally understand the term—but it can also mean "evangelical" in the more general sense. For the sake of consistency, "evangelical" has been used throughout to avoid confusion.

come close to the challenges posed by Mark, who, with his Gospel, wanted to begin a story that we would continue in our own lives. Thus he challenges those who read his work to become "evangelical."

When I began writing this book, I wanted to be guided by the Gospel of Mark to encounter the six anonymous women on a deeper level. At first my dialogue with them was somewhat playful and light. I enjoyed coming into direct contact with these different women and receiving fictitious letters from them in reply, and it brought a charm and esprit that comes with first getting to know someone. On more intensive engagement with them, however, I increasingly realized the seriousness of the topics that these women demanded through their exemplary behavior. I became aware of how much we can learn from them and what significance they have for us today as disciples of the Lord. Each of them is a "doctor of the church" with high authority to teach because this authority was conferred on them by Jesus himself. Consequently, my relationship with them became still more intense. Based on the Gospel, these women also appealed ever more strongly to my conscience to address many provocative topics within the church, knowing well that this could only happen associatively and even spark disputes! As I continued to think about it, more and more actual persons came to mind along with experiences from my pastoral work that reflect these women's situations and communicate the Gospel scenes in contemporary terms. Thus it may initially appear to be a disadvantage that I'm able to consider things only within the limited framework of my geographical location and my concrete experience. However, this, in turn, is in line with our Benedictine vow of stability and corresponds with the instruction of the angel that the women met at the tomb on Easter: "He is going ahead of you to Galilee; there you will see him" (Mark 16:7). The open ending of Mark's Gospel makes clear: Galilee can just as well be a village in Germany or a small town in the Midwestern United States, and despite its provinciality, it can have relevance for the church throughout the world. That, too, is something I've learned from the women whom Jesus meets in Galilee and Jerusalem: "Wherever the good news is proclaimed in the whole world, what she has done will be told in remembrance of her" (Mark 14:9). These words of appreciation that Jesus speaks of the woman at Bethany can, with no problem, be applied as well to all the other anonymous women. In turn, I sensed that even if I wanted to, I could no longer avoid these women with their provocative words and deeds that are as relevant for us here and now as they were in first-century Palestine. They are a key component of the good news that we are called to proclaim, recalling my niece's wake-up call that I quoted at the beginning of the book: "You sleepyhead…Stand up!"

Throughout this process I was encouraged that even St. Benedict, the founder of our order, was provoked by a woman at the end of his life. I would like to conclude this book by considering this reassuring story.

Pope Gregory the Great (540–604), who composed Benedict's biography, reports that Benedict used to meet his beloved sister, Scholastica, once a year for spiritual conversation. In order to do this he had to leave his monastery on Monte Cassino and descend to a property at the foot of the mountain. This may already be a first indication that he was led by his sister into a profound faith. The two siblings spent the entire day in spiritual conversation in a small house. When evening came, Benedict rose to leave in order to follow the *Rule*'s instruction that he return to the monastery punctually before sundown. Scholastica, however, implored him, "I beg you. Do not leave me alone this night, so that we can continue to speak of the joys of the heavenly life until morning!" But Benedict stood his ground and strongly reprimanded his sister: "What are you saying, sister? In no way can I remain outside the monastery." It was a bright, beautiful day with no clouds in the sky. Disappointed by her brother's dismissive words, Scholastica laid her head down and tearfully prayed to God. Just then, an intense thunder and lightning storm arose and a huge cloudburst came down so Benedict couldn't leave the house. Seeing the weather, he complained, "May almighty God forgive you, sister! What have you done?" To which Scholastica retorted, "See, I begged you and you didn't hear me; so I prayed to my Lord, and he heard me. Go now, if you can. Leave me and return to your monastery!"

Of course, it was impossible for Benedict to leave the house, and so the siblings passed the night together in prayer and spiritual conversation. Early in the morning Benedict returned to his monastery, and three days later he learned that his sister had died. Pope Gregory concludes this profound episode by commenting that Scholastica could do more because she loved more.

At the end of his life Benedict learned from his sister what it means to love: the person and their well-being is central, not obedience to rules. This, in turn, fully corresponds to Jesus's acts of healing.

This story touches me anew again and again, and every year I must smile a bit when we get together with a community of Benedictine sisters in Munich to celebrate the Feast of St. Scholastica. One of the prayers says, about the relationship between the two siblings, that Benedict was Scholastica's teacher and she learned from him. Pope Gregory says nothing about this. They were mutually involved in the exchange of spiritual ideas, and at the end of his life, it was Benedict who was taught by Scholastica. Even if her name means "pupil," she was for him a teacher. Sometimes I ask myself whether the text of this prayer came from a man's pen. Unfortunately, I don't know the answer.

For me, therefore, Scholastica takes her place in the line of the anonymous women whom St. Mark the Evangelist presents to us as exemplary disciples of Jesus. Like them, she is a pupil of the Teacher and a teacher of the disciples. Thus, something from the scene just described forms a part of the history of how this book came about.

These anonymous women, like Scholastica, have motivated me to leave the security of my monastery. I have carried on an intensive spiritual conversation with them. Through their example they have led me into the depths of the "evangelical" existence of a disciple and they became my teachers. Regarding the challenges to the church in our time and the provocations that they offer, they begged me, along with their contemporaries, "Please don't leave me alone!" And just as boldly as Scholastica they urged me, "Go now, if you can!"

This book, then, is an attempt, based on the Gospel, to bring into the spiritual conversation many current topics concerning the church that we neither can nor should avoid. I have not written it to conjure up intraecclesial cloudbursts with thunder and lightning, and certainly not to make a name for myself by airing provocative topics. Rather, it's much more about the spiritual struggle among siblings who wish to set out together, as *ekklesia*, on the way of life shown by the Lord, with the Gospel for their guide.

Scholastica could do more because she loved more. Benedict learned this through being thwarted by the thunderstorm. In the end, love is what counts! And so, as a sister in faith, she, too, calls out to us: "You sleeper, you tardy one, you sleepyhead, you groundhog!—Stand up!" Being awakened and having to get up aren't always pleasant things—not even for the church. But it is a thoroughgoing Easter event: *ut in omnibus glorificetur Deus* (so that in all things God may be glorified; RB 57.9).